NOW I AM A SWIMMER

Silverdale Holiday Camp

THE FIRST 100 YEARS

Dear Mr Farrar

Thank you for letting me come to Silverdale. I had a nice holiday thank you so can I come again next year. When I was in the swimming pool I was a learner but now I am a swimmer.

Love from Frank

Frances McNeil has written extensively for theatre, radio and television. Her limited edition novel, *Sisters on Bread Street*, set in Leeds around the time of the First World War, will be published in an expanded version by Orion in 2005, entitled *Somewhere Behind the Morning*.

NOW I AM A SWIMMER

Silverdale Holiday Camp

THE FIRST 100 YEARS

FRANCES McNEIL

Pavan
Press

First published in Great Britain in 2004
Pavan Press
PO Box 150
Leeds LS8 3ZP
pavanpress@fastmail.fm

ISBN 0 9525547 2 0

Leeds Children's Holiday Camp Association
6-8 Lower Ground
York Place
Leeds LS1 2DS
Phone/fax 0113 245-4281

Registered Charity No 224649

Contents

Acknowledgements

This book is printed with financial assistance from Leeds City Council.

'Town and Country Child' Copyright 1945, Muriel Levy/Estate of Muriel Levy, permission sought.
'Sunset Reflections,' William Riley, 1957, published by Herbert Jenkins – permission granted by James I C Boyd.
Material from Annual Reports reproduced by permission of Leeds Children's Holiday Camp Association.

Every effort has been made to trace copyright holders. If you have not been asked to give formal permission to include your material, we trust that turning these pages will come as a pleasant surprise.

Photographs courtesy of LCHCA, Yorkshire Post Newspapers, Ross Parry Agency, Leeds Amateur Operatic Society and individuals. Mary Burridge kindly photographed Archive photographs.

Thanks to the committee and staff of LCHCA for keeping excellent records over the years and to the West Yorkshire Archive Service at Sheepscar for making available minutes, cuttings, photographs and correspondence.

BBC Look North, BBC Radio Leeds, the Yorkshire Evening Post, Yorkshire Post, Morecambe Visitor, Lancaster Guardian and Silverdale Parish Magazine alerted people to get in touch with their stories and memories.

'This Goodly House – Its People and Its Times' by Doreen Newlyn, WAC Publications, provided useful insights.

Thanks to everyone who helped in many different ways, including Sue Campbell, E Margaret Dixon, Barbara Newcombe, Stephen Noble, Angela Widdows, Staff at Caring Together in Woodhouse and Little London. Thanks to the Writers' Guild of Great Britain for advice. Patrica McNeil and Rebecca McNeil gave practical assistance. James C McNeil volunteered IT support.

The team at Peepal Tree Press provided valuable guidance on the production of the finished book.

Contributors

Augustine Awonaiy

J. Baxter

Clifton Bingham

Mary Brand

Colin Broadbent

Margaret Bromley (nee Sayles)

Mabel Brooksbank

Ann Brown

James Bucknall

Shona Burke

Iris Crow

J. Dalby

Douglas Dale

L. Dickinson

John Dixon

Roy Dixon

Jean Edwards

Ray Emmerson

Ernest Farrar

Elaine Hartley

Kristina Hazelgrave

Lynne Higo

Charles Jennings

Joyce Leach (nee Greenwood)

Muriel Levy

Lilian Mallory (nee Constantine)

John Markham

Christine Masterman

Mary Morris

Ernest H. Morris

Alan Pinder

Christine Pinkney

Wynifred Price

William Riley

Marjorie Robinson

Milly A Rodgers

Harold Sheffield

Nellie Simpson (nee Kemp)

Mary Smith

Robert Stone

Stanley Thompson

Alan Tomlinson

Yvonne Warburton

G. Wortley

Foreword

By ALAN PINDER, Chairman,

Leeds Children's Holiday Camp Association

When the late, great Ernest Morris asked me to be Treasurer of LCHCA in 1981, I must confess that I had never heard of it, nor indeed of the beautiful village on Morecambe Bay which gives Silverdale Holiday Camp its name. Later on, in 1992, for my pains I became Chairman myself.

So, there have been 23 years of committee meetings, Annual Reports, Treasurer's Reports and the like, and by this time I thought I knew as much about the Camp and the Association as anyone alive, until, that is, I saw the draft of this book …..

It was my wife Jane who first suggested a book about Silverdale, some years back when the Centenary was beginning to loom large. 'Some young history graduate at the University will research it for you, or you could write it yourself', she said. Well, maybe, but so many things, good and not so good have happened to the Association in the last few years that 'the book' and indeed the Centenary itself had to a degree been relegated to the 'back burner'.

Then Frances McNeil came along, with an offer to write such a book, an offer that was readily accepted. Frances was a 'Silverdaler' herself, attending the Camp in the Fifties, and her personal memories and recollections have underpinned this beautifully researched piece of work. Some of the founder members are a long-time dead, but Frances has succeeded in somehow bringing them back to life in these pages. Who can fail to admire the enthusiasm and determination of Helen Briggs or, perhaps stand in awe of her obviously considerable personal resources, when a 'cottage for visitors' is apparently purchased as easily as we would buy a new sofa for the front room! So moving, also, is the author's gentle tribute to the gallant Miss Richardson, who laboured so long for very little reward.

There are of course many unsung heroes in these pages, and it will not have escaped people's notice that the majority of them were women in a predominantly man's world. However, in my time our President has always been a woman, no less a person than the Lady Mayoress of Leeds herself. In closing this foreword, I send greetings to the present incumbent of the post, Mrs Sylvia Taggart, and hope that her successors will continue to be our President as long as Silverdale itself continues.

Leeds, April 2004

Introduction

In 1956, three girls from my school, St. Augustine's, were offered a free two week holiday at Silverdale on the Lancashire coast. My mother jumped at the chance. Margaret's parents gave permission. Ann's mother would have said yes, but her father said no. No daughter of his would be allowed to go to the Leeds Poor Children's Holiday Camp. I didn't care. I was off to the seaside.

It rained and rained. Margaret and I and another girl, whose name I can't now remember, formed a gang of three. Together we produced three pantomimes. For each production, one of us would be The Writer, one would be The Director and one would be The Star. Eager children auditioned for starring roles in 'Jack and the Beanstalk' and 'Cinderella', not knowing it was a carve-up between the three of us. 'Sleeping Beauty' was our final production, and for that Mrs Farrar lent her wedding dress.

Mr Farrar taught me to swim. Not so long ago my mother said she wished she had kept his letter. He wrote to say he had taught me to swim as a thank you for keeping the children occupied on rainy days.

We didn't get within paddling distance of the sea. Mr Farrar feared that we would be lost in quick-sands if we walked onto the beach. As I write, the tragic deaths of Chinese workers, picking cockles in Morecambe Bay, explains Mr Farrar's fears for his charges.

We strolled through woods, and to the village shop to buy sweets. As we passed by in a crocodile, an old man stood still and doffed his trilby hat, the way people did if it was a funeral. I asked Mr Farrar why he had done that. He said the man wanted to show that, in his eyes, we were all as good as the queen.

Mrs Farrar had promised to make toffee, but when we got back it was burnt. We were a little disappointed, but all of us were kids who were used to things going wrong. One little girl spent the whole fortnight asking me to tell her the time from the big clock in the hall. She must have been desperately home-sick.

The Centenary of Leeds Children's Holiday Camp Association gives me the opportunity to learn its history. Who chose that particular spot? - bracing but certainly not bucket and spade territory. How did they keep it going through two world wars and economic depressions? Why has it proved such an enduring part of life in Leeds for a hundred years, and what does the future hold?

The Association kept impressive records going back to the earliest days. Detailed minutes and reports list the name of every person who contributed time, energy, ideas and money. Threepence from an anonymous school child, the proceeds of a band concert, a cheque from an MP or the proceeds of Flag Day - it's all noted and appreciated. Committee meetings across the years held a moment's silence for those who, after years of sterling work, floated off to the Great Holiday Camp in the Sky. At first, I started to jot down the names of people who deserve to be remembered. Some sat through hundreds of hours of committee meetings. Others mended children's clothing week after week, year after year. I planned to list them, in a roll of honour. I had to give up. It would take encyclopaedic volumes to record the names of the generous people in Leeds, Arnside, Carnforth and Silverdale who in their different ways and with their generous hearts helped give Leeds children a century of holidays by the sea.

THE EARLY DAYS

In 1905 Leeds Poor Children's Holiday Camp Association looked back on its first successful year of sending Leeds children to the seaside. Among the band of people present in the Town Hall, two women were to remain linked to the holiday camp for the rest of their lives: Mrs Helen Currer Briggs (Helen Briggs, as she signed herself) and Miss M E Richardson.

Miss M E Richardson already had a part-time job. Her work with Leeds Invalid Children's Aid Association gave her a 'thorough and practical knowledge of the class of people' from which the children came. She was employed by the Poor Children's Holiday Camp Association in the role of 'Enquiry Officer' at a salary of Twenty five pounds a year, payable quarterly. Her job title later changed to Organising Secretary. Notebook in pocket, pencil behind her ear, she caught trams and wore out shoe leather tramping tightly packed narrow streets of red brick back-to-back houses, courts and tenements from York Road to Woodhouse and from Burmantofts to Beeston Hill. Her task was to investigate every case and to check the wages (if any) of the parents. Were the families poor enough for their children to qualify for a free holiday? They were. By the standards of the time, based on surveys in London and York, the families were below the poverty line.

A complaint regarding a girl who had been turned down was rejected because the family income was between £1-15-0 and £1-18-0 (£1.75 to £1.80) per week.

The families who benefited had incomes of considerably less than a pound a week and many hungry mouths.

Low wages, a downturn in trade, unemployment, sickness, the death of a breadwinner, too many mouths to feed – any or all of these - and a family could tumble into destitution and stay there for a lifetime. Britain, workshop of the world and heart of the Empire, was a nation of rich and desperately poor.

Speaking in 1910, Dr Cameron, Medical Officer of Health for the city, said that more than one-fifth of the children born in South-east Leeds died during their first year: 215 deaths of children under one year out of every

During 1908 '1,515 solid pounds of flesh had been added to the 674 children who went to the Camp, and all for the total outlay of £692 11s 3d. In other words, two pounds weight had been added for every £1 spent.'

Annual Report

Districts of Leeds

From which Children sent to Camp have been drawn.

—York Road, York Street, Marsh Lane, Quarry Hill and the Bank	157
II—Burmantofts, Newtown, Mabgate, Leylands	73
III—Hunslet District	94
IV—Holbeck and Beeston Hill	67
V—Armley and Wortley	76
VI—Kirkstall and Burley	59
VII—West Street and Wellington Road	30
VIII—Woodhouse and Camp Road	94
Total number sent to Camp, 1911	650

Wage Average.

	£	s	d
650 children have been taken from 505 families to Camp.			
Total sum of money earned by 505 families	316	2	8
Giving an average wage per family per week of		12	6
This income has to cover house rent, food and clothing, &c., for 3,154 persons comprising these families, per head per week		2	0

1,000, as compared with 118 deaths per 1,000 in then well-to-do Chapeltown.

Helen Briggs had proved an able Lady Mayoress in 1903-1904. Alderman Mr Arthur Currer Briggs, J.P. died in 1906. His death may have prompted his widow to devote so much of her future time and energy to the Charity they had nurtured together during her husband's year of office.

The idea of forming the Camp was taken to the Lady Mayoress by Mr J S R Phillips, Dr Algernon Wear and Mr W H Platts. A description of Helen Briggs' daughter Helen in Doreen Newlyn's 'This Goodly House' seems to match the mother too. 'She was a gifted, cultivated and creative woman with considerable energy'. A Unitarian, Helen Briggs was active at Mill Hill Chapel, President of the Women's League of Unitarian and other Free Christian Churches and a delegate to a conference in America.

She was a member of the Yorkshire Ladies Council of Education, and took an interest in the Gentlewomen's Employment Scheme, the Association for Friendless Girls and the Society for the Prevention of Cruelty to Children. She also helped to establish the Leeds Maternity Hospital. As President of the Choir Committee and a member of the Leeds Musical Festival Committee, she still found time for music and sociability. Mother of two sons and a daughter, in November 1905 she invited the entire Camp Committee to celebrate her daughter's birthday at a tea to be held in the People's Hall.

The Currer-Briggs had money by the bucket load. Mr Currer-Briggs' cash came from coal. When he died, the Colliery Company erected a 'commodious recreation hall' for the villagers of Whitwood in his memory.

- - LEEDS - -

Poor Children's Holiday Camp Association.

OFFICERS FOR 1906.

Chairman:
MRS. BRIGGS.

Honorary Treasurer:
CHARLES TURNER, ESQ.

Hon. Medical Examiner:
DR. MCGREGOR YOUNG.

Honorary Secretaries:
MISS LORNA BARRAN.
DR. ALGERNON WEAR.   REV. C. S. DUNN.

Committee:

MR. J. S. R. PHILLIPS.	MISS NICHOLS.
SIR JOHN BARRAN, BART.	MR. O. CONNELLAN.
MR. H. J. ROWLING.	MRS. R. HUDSON.
PROFESSOR R. M. CONNAL.	MAJOR TARRY.
MRS. H. G. NIXON.	MR. SHORTLAND.
MRS. CHARLES TURNER.	MISS E. KITSON.
MR. J. TETLEY.	MR. G. W. PEACE.
MRS. HAMPSHIRE.	MRS. HAWKYARD.

And the Officers as mentioned above.

Local Committee:

MISS BATE.	REV. W. AND MRS. SLEIGH.
MISS R. BATE.	REV. H. GAMBLE.
REV. R. H. AND MRS. LAW.	MAJOR SAUNDERS, J.P.
DR. AND MRS. GROVENOR.	MR. AND MRS. HAMILTON.
MISS CROSSLEY.	MR. F. L. O'DWYER.
	(Local Hon. Sec. Arnside.)

Enquiry Agent:
MISS RICHARDSON.

OFFICE: 32, GREAT GEORGE STREET, LEEDS.

---

*M*y mother, born 1908, was illegitimate and was put in a home in Leeds called Leeds Ladies Association for the Care and Protection of Friendless Girls which ran from 1884-1944, in Hanover Square in Leeds.

I always remember her telling me that she was sent to the holiday camp, either at Hest Bank or Silverdale, for one week and she said one week was for boys and the next for girls.

About half way through her week there, she and some other girls were standing on the swings inside a building, trying to see who could touch the ceiling first, while the swing was moving. She fell off, got concussion, and when she woke up the girls had gone home and the boys were there, so she didn't have much of a holiday, and because of what she had done, the matron at the time in the orphanage would not let her go again.

How old my mother was when she went to the camp, I don't know, but her name at that time would have been Amy Briggs. She was always sorry she didn't get her full holiday there, or the chance to go again.

J Dalby (Mrs)

Children from the age of seven to thirteen went to the camp for two weeks – boys one fortnight, girls the next. By arrangement with the Education Committee, they gathered at Czar Street School, Holbeck on a Saturday, and changed into the clothing provided. Girls wore dark blue dresses and red tam-o'-shanters or straw hats; boys corduroy trousers, blue jerseys and red caps. The children were provided with clogs, regarded as being more serviceable than boots, and cloaks for wet and cold weather. The boys' and girls' own clothing was stored in cupboards at the school. Dr McGregor Young examined the children, to make sure they had no contagious diseases or head lice.

Mr Arthur Greenwood and Mr Thorpe weighed each child before and after the holiday, and kept statistics up to date. Weight gains were regarded as evidence of the efficiency of the diet and the benefits of the holiday. The children were given a hot dinner before being taken to the railway station to meet the camp superintendent, Mr Tom Wilson, who would have brought back the previous group of children earlier that day. Tom Wilson wore a navy blue suit (one extra pair of trousers provided) and 'a cap showing his connection with the scheme'.

Two babies, dog and friend

Centre Tom Wilson

WEIGHT STATISTICS.

	lbs.
Increase in weights in 37 Boys, from August 26th to September 9th	151¾
Increase in weights in 29 Girls, from September 9th to September 23rd...	88½
Increase in weights in 37 Boys, from September 23rd to October 7th ... ... ·· ...	137
Increase in weights in 26 Girls, from October 7th to October 21st ... ... ·· ...	98
	475

Average increase in each child ... 3½ lbs.

Largest increase—Newman Barnet, aged 9 years,
  On going to Camp weighed ... ... 2 st. 1½ lbs
  On return from Camp weighed ... ... 3 ,, 1¼ ,,
    Increase ... 13¾ lbs.

Next largest— Herbert Booth, age 8 years,
  On going to Camp weighed ... .. 3 st. 11 lbs
  On return from Camp weighed ... ... 4 ,, 5 ,,
    Increase ... 8 lbs.

Nelly Linley, aged 14½ years,
  On going to Camp weighed ... ... 4 st. 12 lbs
  On return from Camp weighed ... ... 5 ,, 5½ ,,
    Increase ... 7½ lbs.
(The normal weight of a girl this age is 7 st. 6 lbs.)

One child (Ethel Wilkinson) lost ½ lb.

Annual Report 1906

The children travelled by train from Wellington Street Station. A Yorkshire Evening News journalist wrote that the girls had a concert on the train, singing all the popular songs. They changed at Carnforth for Arnside, and cheered when they saw the sea. The train left Leeds at 2.15 pm and the girls arrived at the camp at 6 o'clock.

As well as Mr and Mrs Wilson and their helpers, a local visiting committee supervised the holiday. After an initial uneasiness in and around Arnside and Silverdale at the influx of so many city children, members of the local church brought gifts. Dr Dixon, Dr Grosvenor of Arnside and later Dr Barnes of Silverdale could be called on for medical attention.

Local people, including the Edmonds sisters, went to the Camp to play the piano and sing with the children and to tell stories. There is a sense of good comradeship and new friendships among the volunteers. Miss Bulmer seemed to travel across from Leeds specially to put on teas. When the camp was unoccupied, a good neighbour from Arnside, Mr Newsham, supervised the buildings.

During the stay at camp, the 'very few' rules had to be kept to the letter. All children must be obedient to the superintendent. All must faithfully perform the household duties required of him or her. In 1907 when Dr Wear visited the camp, he was struck by the amount of hard work the children had to do. The committee agreed that the children should do only light work, with six different children helping daily, though on the last day they must all help to clean the camp.

Ideals of self-improvement, orderliness, cleanliness, purity and 'training' in domestic tasks for both boys and girls were regarded as part of the wider benefit to the city as a whole. The Chief Constable of Leeds noted that in 1910 there had been 410 first offenders in the city. He declared that no more 'first offender' recruits were wanted. In 'stopping the supply at source', the police boss knew of no better agency than the Association.

Helen Briggs wished she could give each child a financial start in life. She did not achieve this grand ambition, but there were letters of gratitude, and requests for employment. Many boys and girls were helped by the committee to get work. One boy got a job at the Yorkshire Post – not surprising since the paper's J S R Phillips was the first Chairman of the Association.

The Association had its critics. In 1908, Dr William Hall complained that the camp promoted divine discontent. He came across one girl who was well-known to him. Two weeks after coming back from camp this fatherless girl with a drunkard for a mother was being punished at school for insubordination. He saw no physical improvement in her. She was unclean, and the clothing she had been given the previous winter was dirty

Dear Madam :

I thank the Committee for what they did for Walter at the Holiday Camp. It did him a lot of good and built him up. If he had been away another two or three weeks we should not have known him.

H.W.

and ragged. She told the doctor she had learnt the skirt dance at the camp but refused to give him a demonstration.

He said that two weeks of happiness only made her more aware of her fifty weeks of misery – being ill-fed, poorly clothed and badly housed. Dr Hall praised a school near East End Park where children were provided with some holiday activity and went home each night. He also said that he had weighed truants at the two industrial schools, where children would be sent if they failed to attend school. There they were fed and trained. These children were heavier by a pound or two than 'the little fools who in obedience to their parents or the school Attendance Officer go regularly to the ordinary schools in the poorer parts of the city.' The doctor longed for the dawn of an era of justice. He believed that good feeding should take place in schools and if a child showed mental aptitude it should be transferred to another school where it might study at a higher level. Dr Hall thought it sickening that feeding children should be left to charity.

Helen Briggs hoped that the sunshine, fresh air, happiness, good food and change of scenery would make the young folks dissatisfied. This was one of their aims. If the young became dissatisfied, they would strive with might and main for a better future. Miss Richardson tried humour – 'To do the skirt dance, one must first have a skirt, just as Mrs Glass advised that you must first catch your hare'. She added that skirt dancing was not taught at the camp. Many of the girls were employed in pantomimes in the winter months and probably taught each other dancing.

But Dr Williams had a valid point. Constant hunger was a serious problem. A deputation of working men attended the Association's committee meeting in late 1904 and asked that the Association give the poor children of Leeds a free meal during the coming winter. The committee sympathised but felt they could not use funds for that purpose without calling subscribers together. Helen Briggs undertook to call a meeting in the Lord Mayor's rooms to set up a scheme for feeding destitute children during the coming winter.

Members of the Committee visit the camp

Staff

15

PHOTO BY FRANK CROSLAND   ARNSIDE

TIME TABLE.

7-0 a.m.	Get up, wash and dress.
8-0 "	Breakfast.
10-30 "	Drill, and play, and house duties.
12 noon	Dinner.
2 to 4 p.m.	Games, etc.
4.30 "	Tea.
7.30 "	Supper.
8.30 "	Bed.

Czar Street School, Holbeck

Wellington Street Station

July 14th 1914

Letter from **Mary Morris** to the Committee

This is my second time here, but it is four years since I was here last, and I have been anxiously waiting for the time to arrive, for I knew it was a beautiful place.

We go out for long walks with Mr Wilson and the other children and often see many sights, such as the Tower which is now in ruins.

The bedroom windows are opened in the morning, and kept so all day, so as to let the rooms get plenty of air in them for when we go to bed.

All this is done by Mrs Wilson, and we should all be obedient to show our kindness for all she does for us. All the rooms are well ventilated and are kept clean and tidy.

Several of the girls do portions of cleaning in the dining-room and bedrooms, and also make the beds and scrape potatoes.

I do a part of the dining-room every day, and help to wash up the pots and plates which are used for breakfast.

In the fields round about the Camp grow nuts and gooseberries which we gathered one day when we were out. We also gathered flowers to put in the dining-room.

We can run about and play as much as we like about the fields, and bathe in the sea sometimes when the tide is out. The tide is lovely to watch when it comes in and out, and see the foam rising to the surface.

In the spot named the Northern Riviera, Arnside Knott protected the Camp from the north and north-east winds. The opening of the bay towards the south and west gave the camp a sunny aspect – when the sun co-operated. The geological foundations in the area consist of limestone, which does not hold water. With no possibility of wells or springs, the camp relied on tanks of rain-water. One Leeds Lord Mayor declared it to be one of the healthiest neighbourhoods in the British Isles. But how did they arrive at that particular spot?

One model for the Leeds Association was the Manchester and Salford Street Children's Mission at St. Anne's, on the Lancashire coast. Other camps were set up by boys' clubs and church brigades. When discussions were first being held about setting up a holiday venture, Hull Boys' Club wrote to the Leeds Committee enclosing their report and balance sheet. Halifax lads always went to Filey and used tents. One committee member gave particulars of a camp that had opened in summer 1903 in Scarborough. Helen Briggs followed up information about a site between Saltburn and Redcar. A site was offered at St. Anne's at five shillings a year. Cleethorpes and Bridlington were suggested, and a visit made to Fleetwood. On 12th June, 1904, Helen Briggs reported on two splendid sites at Silverdale: one of them the 'deserted village', with the remains of some old houses and a well. A quarry site at Jenny Brown's point was considered as a temporary site for 1904 – to have a wooden hut supplemented by tents. The decision was left to the sites sub-committee to choose between Jenny Brown's point and a bunga-low at Hest Bank. They plumped for Hest Bank. The tent that held beds was not big enough for playing in on wet days, so Helen Briggs rented Mrs Atkinson's field adjoining the bungalow where a tent for play could be erected. She also arranged with Mrs Atkinson for water to be carried daily to the camp. The summer went smoothly, although the militia camping near Hest Bank had proved 'something of an annoyance'.

On 21st November, 1904 in the Yorkshire Post Board Room, Helen Briggs reported that she had secured a site for five years at Arnside, with the option of a further lease. Dr Wear announced that he had bought the Refresh-ment Room from the Bradford Exhibition at a cost of £53. A local man would dig out the foundations for £40. Removal, carriage and re-building on site would cost £39. Helen Briggs kindly offered to fit up the building with scarlet blinds.

At the first committee meetings there had been talk of joining forces with Bradford to send children on holiday but this did not hap-pen. A year later, the Leeds committee were worrying about the Bradford Cinderella Soci-ety's camp at Hest Bank. The Bradford super-intendent was said to be an 'aggressive atheist', had no control over the children and the camp was 'dirty and neglected'. People might think that this was the Leeds camp. Dr Wear would write to the Cinderella Society, after Helen Briggs had made further enquiries.

FROM THE SLUMS.

TO THE SEA

THE FIRST WORLD WAR

In 1914 the formal opening of the Camp took place on June 20th. The children had a 'happy day' and the Lord and Lady Mayoress and the Committee and friends from Leeds and Arnside enjoyed their outing.

Two months later, with the outbreak of war, the camp was closed. The buildings were offered as a hospital for the wounded. The Base Hospital in Leeds said the offer would be accepted if needed. The Camp was also offered as a training centre for recruits, or a hostel for Belgian refugees. For various reasons the offers were not accepted. The result was that fewer children were sent to camp that year: 534 children (242 boys and 292 girls) had a holiday – 179 less than in 1913.

The camp was lent for six weeks to the Committee of the Children's Summer Holiday Fund. This was an organisation that charged for holidays and had their country homes in the East Riding of Yorkshire. It was considered unwise to send the children there because of war conditions. In December 1914, the German fleet had bombarded Scarborough, Whitby and Hartlepool and laid mines off the coast.

Dr Whalley, who had examined the children before their departure to camp, answered his country's call and was serving at the front with the Royal Army Medical Corps. Dr Legge took his place for a short time before joining up himself.

Miss Richardson visited the homes of sixty Camp boys on the Roll of Honour. Many had been wounded. Some were 'well again' and had gone back to France. In 1916, two had fallen: John Hardwick and Clifford Marsden.

The Committee are proud and happy to record that several of their old Camp boys are serving in the Army and Navy. We have already on our Roll of Honour 49 boys, and the Committee feel sure there are many more if only we could get in touch with them. Any other names the Committee will be glad to receive.

ROLL OF HONOUR.

Laurence Abrams.	John E. Page.	Arthur Beaumont.
Jackson Abrams.	Albert Lockwood.	Vincent Walsh.
George Schofield.	John W. Harrison.	Bernard Walsh.
John Robinson.	Willie Dunn.	John E. Casey.
Edward Roach.	Peter Dunn.	Joe Clegg.
Arthur Riley.	Frank Fox.	John W. Hepworth.
Mark Lee.	Robert Sanderson.	James Newton.
Walter Beasley.	Thomas Widdop.	Percy Milner.
Harry Milner.	Norman Hollings.	John Madden.
Albert Hollings.	John Madden.	Mark Degnan.
Joseph Madden.	Sam Butterfield.	Joseph Morris.
William Hardy.	Robert Hawley.	William Moir.
George Goodwin.	William Morris.	William Kay.
Joseph Doolan.	Robert Worthington.	John Hardwick.
William Hardwick.	Harry Hardwick.	George Hawkhead.
Jeremiah Ford.	Joseph Dobson.	Sam Smith.
	William Ott.	

1916

THE CHILDREN'S NEED

From highway and bye-way, and dark, dismal alley,

    The cry of the children comes shrill on the breeze,

They long for a glimpse of the hillside and valley,

    The fields and the flowers, and leaf-laden trees.

Those wan, weary faces proclaiming the story

    Of poverty, sorrow, of sadness and woe,

Of lives spent in darkness, and wanting the glory

    Of sunshine and gladness to cheer as they go.

Children of men, who, maybe, fight the battle

    Of Empire on fields far away from their kin,

And yet spare a thought 'mid the roar and the rattle

    For bairnies, whose cry they can hear thro' the din.

Shall we forget them? enjoying our pleasure;

    Or shall we remember? and help to impart

A feeling so joyous, in o'er-flowing measure,

    That earth becomes Heaven to each youthful heart.

They're somebody's bairns, though forlorn, poor and lonely,

    A'thirsting for sunlight and God's pure, fresh air;

Then generously give of your bounty, if only

    To make for a while their vision more fair.

The boys and the girls of to-day must be cared for,

    Their young lives made happy, and helped in the strife,

That they in the coming years may be prepared for

    The strenuous work in the battle of Life.

April, 1915.   J. BAXTER.

*The above lines are specially written for the
Leeds Poor Childrens' Holiday Camp Association.*

I was seven when the war started. My father was in the army. Being the eldest I had quite a bit to do to help my mum. I scrubbed floors, helped with the washing, queued for stuff, like margarine – and there was none!

I'll be 97 this year, but I can see it now. I got into trouble for running too far along the beach. And I asked for more sweetener on our porridge. I was a bit of a rebel. I would dare things, be a darer.

I didn't like it at Silverdale. We were too regimentated, like a little army. When we came back we were thoroughly weighed at Great George Street.

I got back to my own life, helping my mum. I joined the queues for food and saw a lot of men who had been badly injured in the war, lost an arm or a leg.

Wynifred Price

This year the Committee are making a special effort to send to the Camp the needy children of our soldiers and sailors who have fallen in battle, or who are now at the front fighting for their country; also Belgian Refugee children now resident in the city.

Produced on thin wartime paper, the Association's fourteenth Annual Report, 1918, records that although many of the 'poorer classes' have obtained additional earnings through war work, the need for the free annual holiday for the children of the poorest had not lessened. Funds had decreased, and so in the summer of 1917 only 256 children went to camp, as against 526 in 1916, 534 in 1912, and 837 in 1910. Almost all the summer 1917 children had fathers who had been killed or maimed in the war. By 1917, almost a hundred boys who had holidayed at the Camp were serving in the Army or Navy.

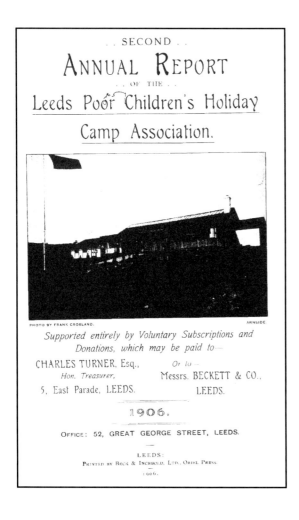

Dr F. Whalley D.S.O. returned from war service and took up the post of Honorary Secretary. Dr A. Wear C.M.G. became Vice Chair. Mrs Briggs was awarded an M.B.E., for her work with wounded soldiers at her hospital 'Broadleys', Windermere. She equipped an operating theatre at Beckett Park Hospital for wounded soldiers, and continued as Chairman of the Camp Committee.

After the war, the Committee were full of ideas and plans, some of which have still not come to pass. Leeds needed a small, bright, happy hospital for children. Child welfare organisations would do more good if amalgamated. The benefits of the National Insurance Scheme, which went to those in work, should also go to children. One bright spot for Helen Briggs was that for the first time since the National Society for the Prevention of Cruelty to Children came to the city, no cruelty case was brought before the magistrates.

Expensive structural repairs to the Camp were planned for 1919, but fate intervened. The Camp burnt to the ground.

Camp destroyed by fire

They are puny, sometimes ragged, head to feet.
And their playground is the pavement or the street ;
    And their little faces plead
    For your help and for your heed,
And their thin hands make your heart with pity beat.

Be it much or be it little that you do,
'Tis a deed of love your heart will never rue,
    Their young laughter will arise
    To the ever list'ning skies
Like a song of praise and thanksgiving to you!

                CLIFTON BINGHAM.

Photo by Bacon.   THE OFFICE LEEDS   *Leeds.*

The Beach Boys and dog

A LAND FIT FOR HEROES?

The year 1919 has been one of misfortune and sorrow. On Easter Tuesday, April 22nd, the Camp Buildings at Far Arnside were totally destroyed by fire, caused by a neighbouring farmer setting fire to the gorse in spite of warnings that such a procedure would endanger the Camp Buildings. Though insured, the destruction was so complete as to necessitate an entirely new building and equipment. A considerable sum has, owing to law proceedings, been promised towards the loss by the farmer, but this will not meet the necessary sum required for reinstatement. A whole beautiful summer's happiness and health has thus been lost to the children.

Annual Report

'Contemplate the future and you will realise that it holds nothing without the child.'

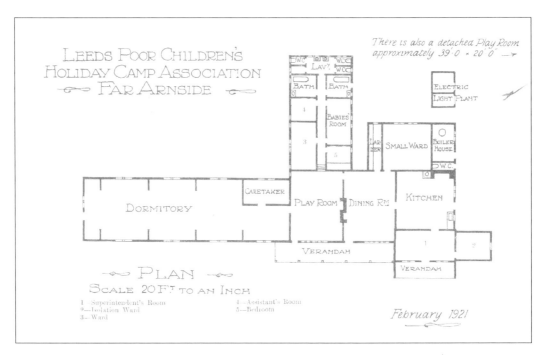

Helen Briggs gave a new building to the Association. Promises of help in money and kind poured in.

There is something almost frantic in the speed with which re-building was accomplished. Helen Briggs wanted the new camp to be regarded as a thank-offering, and also as a memorial to the Camp boys fallen in the war. She took a fifteen year lease on 10½ acres of land near the old site, south-west of Arnside Knott. New and larger buildings

covered 136 feet by 72 feet. They comprised 'four dormitories, playroom, dining room, kitchen, sitting and bedrooms for the staff, bathroom and lavatories with an excellent system of drainage'. An isolation ward was added, in case of need. Fortunately the old playroom remained untouched by the fire. Mrs Briggs donated a small bungalow where people interested in the Association would be able to stay when visiting the camp for a few days.

Thanks to mild weather and heated buildings, between September 10th and December 4th 1920, 314 children, 151 girls and 161 boys, enjoyed a holiday in the new Camp.

In 1921 the isolation ward proved necessary. An outbreak of scarlet fever occurred shortly after the arrival of the last group of girls in October. Prompt action by Dr Jackson of Carnforth, the Honorary Medical Officer at the Camp, Mr and Mrs Wilson and 'skilled assistance' from Leeds prevented the spread of the disease. The patients were taken to Kendal Hospital. All the children stayed an extra week at camp, to make sure they were clear of the disease. The committee member who loved statistics was alive and well. He, or she, demonstrated that the additional week spent at the camp led to an increase in weight of 42 per cent more than for girls who had spent only the usual two weeks at the Camp. Furthermore, a comparison was made between the weight gained by children whose behaviour was 'good' and those whose behaviour was 'bad'. Good children put on more weight. Could this be, the statistician wondered, a case of laugh and grow fat?

Today we worry about childhood obesity. In 1923 the problem was diagnosed as chronic bad health of children from poor families in big cities like Leeds. Dr Wear, Schools Medical Officer, said that an enormous number of children in Leeds schools were suffering defective health. Many children were from 13 to 25 lbs below the weight for their age. The problem was not simply poverty. Parents had not been trained to feed their children properly, according to Dr Wear. Leeds ought to recognise that it would save money in the long run if children were properly fed.

In 1923, the condition of the children on examination before the holiday was distinctly worse than the year before, probably owing to the scarcity of food available because of unemployment. A considerable proportion of children, aged between seven and twelve years old, weighed no more than three stones. In that year, holidays started on Saturday 5th May and the last 'batch' return on Saturday 17th November.

Conduct at Camp.

Batches	Excellent	V. Good	Good	Bad	V. Bad	Total
1st, Girls	6	9	25	...	...	40
2nd, Boys	3	10	25	3	...	41
3rd, Girls	4	14	24	...	...	42
4th, Boys	2	11	28	1	...	42
5th, Girls	5	12	21	2	...	40
6th, Boys	1	11	28	1	1	42
7th, Girls	...	19	37	...	...	56
8th, Boys	1	3	34	8	...	46
9th, Girls	...	15	45	...	...	60
10th, Boys	...	16	39	3	...	58
11th, Girls	...	9	47	3	...	59
12th, Boys	...	9	46	6	...	61
13th, Girls	...	8	34	...	...	42
14th, Boys	...	5	36	4	...	45
	22	151	469	31	1	674

MEALS CHART.

BREAKFAST.
Porridge and Treacle. Milk. Bread.

DINNER.
SUNDAY. Roast Beef, Yorkshire Pudding, Rice Pudding, Potatoes.

MONDAY. Hash, Shepherd's Pie, or Cold Beef, Jam Roll.

TUESDAY. Irish Stew and Potatoes. Bread and Butter Pudding.

WEDNESDAY. Liver and Bacon, or Tripe, Treacle Pudding

THURSDAY. Hot-Pot with Vegetables. Sago Pudding

FRIDAY. Fish and Potatoes. Suet Pudding with Treacle.

SATURDAY. Scotch Broth made of Neck of Mutton, Boiled Raisin Pudding

TEA.
Bread and Butter or Jam, and Cocoa.

SUPPER.
Bread and Treacle, Dripping, Milk

Bradford-born novelist William Riley, then managing director of a firm of optical lantern slide makers, spent a holiday in Grange-over-Sands in 1912. There he revised his manuscript 'Windyridge' He was unsure about the title. Windyridge was adopted as a name for houses of Englishmen all over the world. He need not have worried. The novel sold more than half a million copies. William Riley moved to Silverdale in 1919.

Sunset Reflections

A new interest awaited me that was to bring me a great deal of pleasure for many years, and still does. On one of my earliest rambles, within a very short distance of my home and just within the Westmorland border I had seen a structure erected on the cliffs, and a hundred yards or so from the main road to Arnside, that was described on a board at the entrance gates as "The Leeds Poor Children's Holiday Camp".

The building was a low one, constructed of wood and corrugated iron; to put it mildly, it added nothing to the beauty of the land-scape. All the same, it served a very useful purpose, for during the summer months a succession of children, groups of fifty girls and boys, from the big city's poorest homes, were provided with a fortnight's holiday by the generosity of a voluntary Association.

With the good genius of the movement - a wealthy Leeds lady who was devoted to the children and who had secured their affection, Mrs. Currer Briggs - I soon became ac-quainted, and I was invited to act as honorary local Secretary. To see 'three score light-hearted youngsters at play within the wooden palings that marked the boundaries of the extensive grounds was an entertaining sight. Thereafter for some thirty years it was my privilege to arrange; and more - often than not to conduct, an hour's religious service on the Sunday afternoon in one of the rooms where there was a piano; and the hearty singing of such well-known children's hymns as "Jesus bids us shine" and "All things bright and beautiful" provides a memory that still occasions me genuine pleasure.

The order of service was nondenomina-tional and had the approval of the various religious authorities in the city. The children themselves added to the interest by reciting portions of Scripture, of which the one most frequently quoted was, as might be expected, the twenty-third Psalm. Occasionally one of the children would contribute to the amuse-ment of us older folk, as when one girl concluded the recital by saying, with consid-erable emphasis on the first three words

"Surely to goodness mercy shall follow me all the days of my life, and I will dwell in the house of the Lord for ever."

The misquotation, alas, passed unnoticed by the children.

Looking on those little ones week by week, watching them at their games, and seeing how their faces lit up when a visitor took an interest in them-a *real* interest-was to experience a genuine warming of the heart. The most thrilling occasion was when Mrs. Currer Briggs paid the Camp a visit. How the kiddies flocked round her! How they com-peted for a smile-a hand-touch! I was often reminded of Masefield's lines

". . . he who gives a child a treat
Makes joybells ring in Heaven's street;
And he who gives a child a home Builds palaces in Kingdom come."

William Riley

Lilian Constantine did not hear the joybells ring.

> *I was born in 1912 and went to Quarry Mount School. I was sent to Silverdale between the ages of 10 and 14. It was a free holiday but a rough do. You got your orders after breakfast. I had to get down on my knees and wash the floor. It was a forced holiday. I was the eldest girl and had two older brothers. In those days we were forced to do what our parents said. We were in a long hut with beds – along with children from other schools. We did a lot of walking, that's about the only thing we did, walking.*
>
> **Lilian Mallory (nee Constantine)**

Gifts for the Camp in 1924.

Mrs. Currer Briggs—£5 paid for rent of land for Camp; also curtains, extra furniture, and kitchen utensils for bungalow; cinema apparatus, slides and screen, handkerchiefs and towels for the children; also towels for Leeds Office, and curtains, large cupboard in both rooms, and towel rail; oil stove, basket for wool, also wood box with sewing materials.

Generous supplies of excellent dripping throughout the season from the respective proprietors and managers of—The Grand Restaurant, Griffin Hotel, Majestic Restaurant, Conservative Club, Liberal Club, Hotel Metropole, Leeds Club, Albion Place—greatly appreciated.

Messrs. T. Mabane & Sons—large football.
Pygmalion, per Mr. A. Hamilton—parcel of books.
Mrs. Abbott—parcel of table games and tape for bags.
Mrs. Trevor Wood—parcel of books.
The Amalgamated Press, Leeds—illustrated papers.
Mr. Rogers, Silverdale—2 cricket bats and balls.
Miss Jackson, Silverdale—2 fowls.
Miss Dickens, Silverdale—large rocking-horse.
Miss Pickles, Silverdale—hymn-book with music.
Merchant Taylors' School, Liverpool—saddle and bridle for donkey.
Mrs. P. Roscoe and Mrs. W. Roscoe, Leeds—£1, to be spent on the children
Mrs. Sandford, Leeds—70 small prizes given to the children.
Mrs. Sandford—dish, earthenware, sweets, and boot protectors.
Miss Batt, Arnside—2s. 6d., to be spent on the children.
Mr. Buxton, Woodlesford—17 gramophone records.
Miss Patterson, Arnside—old boots and shoes.
Mrs. Bright, Silverdale—36 tennis balls.
Mrs. Bright—use of car and telephone.
Mr. Brotherton, Leeds—seeds for garden.
Mr. Hampshire, Leeds—fruit, etc.
Miss Edmunds, Silverdale—first-aid dressing.
Mr. and Mrs. Barr, Far Arnside—entertaining all staff and 58 children to tea.
Miss D. Jackson—needle-case for dressing room.
Mrs. Brooke—stockings made for the children.
Mrs. Abbott and Mrs. Gamble—making 50 boot bags.
Mrs. Gamble and Mrs. Tindall—knitted 12 pairs of stockings.
Mrs. Pollard—stockings knitted.
Miss Baker and Miss Coward—jerseys mended.
Mill Hill Sewing Party, per Mrs. Prince—garments
Yorkshire Evening Post " Boots for Bairns " Fund, per Mr. Capes—60 pairs of boots and stockings.
Yorkshire Evening Post—books and puzzles for the children.
Messrs. J. Crockatt & Co. Ltd.—cleaning clothing free of charge.
Barlock Typewriting Co.—duplicating letters free of charge.
Messrs. J. Wetherell—brown paper and string.
Mr. H. Jessop, Whitkirk—60 yards of navy blue serge, also 48 pairs boys' knickers and 24 girls' skirts.
Mr. C. Lillie—chocolates.
Mr. J. E. Bedford—copper stock-pot for Camp
Mr. E. R. Phillips—large doll's house.
Misses Passavant—making garments.

In the summer of 1925, an old boy drove up to the camp gates in his own car to show his wife the place 'where he had first known what Happiness is'. Nothing pleased the Committee more than to receive donations from former campers. Assistants helping the superintendent were sometimes drawn from former camper girls and this was found to be successful. Some children were second generation holidaymakers at Silverdale.

From the earliest days, the Association relied on private donations. At the first meeting, on 3rd December, 1903, at the office of the Charity Organisation Society, it was agreed to draw up a circular explaining the scheme and asking for subscriptions. Some of those present made a start.

Mr J N Barran	Five pounds
Mr Turner	Three guineas (£3.15p)
Mr Phillips	Two guineas (£2.10p)
Dr Wear	Two guineas

By March, £166.13.0 had been promised. Each married policeman in the City of Leeds had undertaken to contribute threepence and each single policeman sixpence to the fund. Two members of Leeds Trade Council were asked to join the committee. The railway offered reduced fares.

The Association was supported by Leeds teachers. James Graham, Director of Education, collected from head teachers. The Yorkshire Evening Post Dolls Collection at Alexandra Hall raised £50. Gifts came from Leeds Bowling Club, Leeds Jewish Board of Guardians, Leeds Typographical Society per Mr Musgrave, the Workpeople's Hospital Fund, Melbourne Brewery, Post Office Staff, Roundhay Park Band Committee, York Road Bible Class, the YMCA, Theosophical Society, the Friendless Girls' Committee, Wildblood & Sons, Leeds & District Amalgamated Society of Anglers, the Bowling Club, Sylvian's Operatic and Dramatic Society to equip a bed, Nox Lamp workers, J Petty &

Sons, the Public Assistance Committee, Vickers and Sons and the intriguingly named Roundhay Bohemiam Ladies' Club. Leeds Picture House on Briggate donated £100 worth of tickets. Appropriately enough for an Association obsessed with weighing children, four lots of donations came one year from the weighing machine in Boots Cash Chemist on Bond Street. Flag Day provided a third of the income. One child out of five was paid for by the pennies and shillings given by the people of Leeds on Flag Day. A member of the General Committee and Chairman of Flag Day, Mr F W Sandford was a southerner by origin and perhaps prompted donations from the Yorkshire Society of Southerners.

From its earliest days, the charity was regarded as one of the most useful in Leeds, run by people who had 'warm hearts and sound heads'. Canon Allison called it 'thoughtful philanthropy'. Helen Briggs hated it if the books could not be balanced. But in the early days Alderman Hepton urged the Committee not to be too economical. On the cold and windy day he visited the Camp, the wind had come up through the floor boards. During 1910, shortly after the offices had moved from 52 Great George Street to 24 Great George Street, they were broken into. The Honorary Treasurer thought that the false impression had got abroad that the Association had plenty of money. The 'visitors' didn't get much.

People gave time and skill as well as money. Supporting the Camp was often a family affair. Committee member Mr J C Gration represented the Leeds Industrial Co-operative Society on the General Committee. When he died, his sister, Miss Gration, took his place.

There is a sense of people having a really good time while coining in the cash. Planning was needed to make sure that fund-raising band performances did not clash. Garden fetes, rummage sales, whist drives, a wireless appeal, a postal appeal, the performance of Noel Coward's 'Bitter Sweet' by Leeds Ama-

teurs – all these events raised money. Golfers held a ball at the Astoria where the popular actress Gertrude Lawrence delighted everyone with her 'amusing talk and wonderful knack of extracting money from the guests'. Another year Wilfred Pickles was the big draw.

And still they sometimes had to say, 'the year did not keep itself'. Expenses across the years included adding rooms, installing an electric lighting plant, a drying shed, piped water and later natural gas.

If Flag Day fell on a day when the weather was foul, or there was a test match at Headingley, takings could be severely depleted.

Then, as now, people remembered the Camp in their wills. Such bequests were gratefully received. Windfalls of that kind are always unexpected and, by their nature, cannot be relied upon by those doing the financial planning.

Poor trade and the general strike increased the need for holidays but decreased income.

1925 was the 21st Anniversary of the Camp. The official mayoral opening on 4th July was a celebratory occasion, with Miss Bulmer providing tea, Mr Riley, Miss Edmonds and the Local Committee providing 'a most excellent entertainment, which the children enjoyed immensely.' As Chairman, Helen Briggs presented the Superintendent and his wife with a gold watch each, to mark their twenty-one years of service.

A bronze tablet, paid for by private subscription, was unveiled by the Lord Mayor. It commemorated the occasion and acknowledged the tireless devotion of Helen Briggs who 'from the moment of the inception of the Camp during her year as Lady Mayoress in 1904 has spared no effort to advance the cause of the Camp, and to make it, as the Association now trust that it is, a permanent factor in the promotion of the welfare of the city of Leeds.' Mrs Briggs was later to say that few people understood the phrase 'poor people'. They had not seen the cramped houses, the lack of food and the 'black despair of mothers unable to give their children a chance in life'.

During 1926, the year of the General Strike, 797 children went to camp – 76 fewer than the year before. There had been a reduction in income and on top of that the shortage of coal led to difficulties in heating the buildings and drying clothes.

Helen Briggs was absent through illness during 1929 but was on the platform at Wellington Station as the fifteen thousandth child boarded the train for Silverdale, clutching a box of chocolates from the Lady Mayoress.

In 1930, Miss Richardson completed 25 years as Organising Secretary and was thanked for her services.

Perhaps increasing age and her recent illness doubled Helen Briggs', and the Committee's, determination to ensure the Camp's future. In 1932 the Camp acquired the freehold of the site at Silverdale from the Dallam Tower Estate. They had always felt confident as tenants under Sir Maurice Bromley-Wilson, but with ownership of the site, and the title deeds in their possession, the Trustees of the Association felt 'secure against whatever chances and changes may emerge from the whirligig of time.'

With the deaths of many of its older subscribers, the Association made a new Appeal for Subscribers. During 1933 – the weather was excellent that year - they had sent an even larger than usual number of children to the Camp. The children came back healthy and plumped up. (One enterprising lad managed to go twice – once using his father's name and again using his mother's name!) But the Committee feared numbers would tumble in the following year if they did not find more money. Incomes dropped in the late 1920s and early 1930s, and this affected people's ability or willingness to contribute. The price of food had risen. Fewer children did go in 1934, but this was because at the last minute a number of children were unable to go due to sickness. There had been 'a good deal of sickness' in schools that year.

Peeling spuds

To me it was a penance not a holiday. We were poor at home but happy, and the time spent there was not happy. I hated the clothes we had to wear, the food, also the staff were very strict. I must not forget the toilet block, a long wooden bench with seven holes (dry of course) we called them the seven holes of misery, had a saying for each one. This was the early 1930s, can't remember when because for my sins I had to go a second time to look after a younger sister.

The sea was so far away you needed a telescope to see it, and the day we went on an organised walk, the sea was out, so no luck there.

I suppose now it would be called character building, or "I'm a Celebrity get me out of here". I'm sure it must be better and more modern. Can you book me in?
Marjorie Robinson

In the twenty-four years of its existence the Camp has had very few instances of runaways, and in all cases such escapades have been discreditable neither to the Camp nor the fugitives. The cause has usually been home-sickness, and those who are acquainted with the homes from which the Association's guests come, can well find something pathetic in the desire to return to them before the holiday is ended. In the year under review [1928] the Camp had four runaways, whose imagination had apparently been accidentally fired by some romantic stories told to the children by one of the kind friends of the Camp who was visiting it during a spell of bad weather. These children – girls – were promptly recovered, thanks to the use of the telephone, which had only recently been installed at Camp.

Annual Report

I was born at 22 Temple View, Easy Road, Leeds 9 on 6th July 1922 and had the good fortune to attend a holiday at Silverdale. I would say it would be 1930 or thereabouts. I remember I was about the smallest of the group.

My memories are few but one that stands out is going to Leeds centre taken by an aunt (my mother had died early) and climbing a staircase to the top floor, where we put on the uniform - grey trousers (short), Jersey, cape and cap. I'm sorry I don't know how we travelled (rail or coach).

On arrival we were allocated sleeping accommodation which was in a large black hut. I suppose it would have been ex-military. There would have been a few of them - one was for dining.

Like many others I remember the walk to the Pepperpot, all dressed smartly in capes and caps. We also were treated to an ice cream. One other thing that stuck in my mind was that the field where we played had a lot of mole hills. One day a chap, whether belonging to the camp or not I don't know, he was there to inspect mole traps and one or more were caught and he even showed us how to skin them, which as you can imagine impressed the city boys.

John Markham

Sometimes the comments and judgements jar. The runaway girls trying to return to Leeds would not have thought of themselves as slum-dwellers with homes not worth returning to. Their thoughts would have been of their parents, brothers, sisters and the rhythm and shape of the lives they knew, and missed - in spite of the good that was being done to them.

On June 29th 1936, a ceremony was held to mark the occasion of the 20,000[th] child going to the Camp. It was held at the Civic Hall rather than at the railway station because Helen Briggs had suffered an accident and was able to watch the presentation of fruit flowers from her car. Not long after that, Helen Briggs died. She had been a mover and shaker for the Association since 1903 and in recent years her personal commitment and expenditure had been huge. She and many others involved with the Association believed they were helping to create a better future, a better world for the generations who would come after them.

I was an absolute wimp for the two weeks I was there. I had hoped to go with my own friends but they were not chosen, so that was my first disappointment.

After an endless journey when I guess I was about 9 years old, (sixty years ago) our first job was to write a letter home, about safe arrival. I was unable to get the words down because of my tears, I had never been separated from my Mother, and I was heartbroken, and already homesick. It should have been a holiday of a lifetime for me, as I had never had a family holiday before.

I can laugh about it now. My vivid memories are of singing very sad songs round the stove in the large hut, which only increased my homesickness.

I do not remember taking my own clothes. We were given black gymslips and red jumpers and, I think, navy blue knickers!

The dining room had wooden tables and benches, and after being helpful with some job or other, I was given an extra slice of bread and jam. (I hated jam then) for tea.

I do not remember how we filled the days. I was too miserable to enjoy it; most of the other children had a fantastic time.

The surrounding areas were beautiful. It's just a pity that there is not a pensioner holiday camp, because sixty years later, I would know how to enjoy all the benefits, and I do have a real desire to go back and visit, which one day, I shall hopefully.

I am really laughing as I write this, it's a shame that I could not laugh then!

Jean Edwards

I went to Silverdale camp 70 years ago (I am now 81). We went from the offices in Great George Street by charabanc. When we arrived the first thing we had to do was get in the large bath, after that we had to de-lice everybody's hair, what a sight that was. I was a bit older than some of the girls so me and the older girls had a dormitory for eight, the smaller girls were in large dormitories.

We were given new clothes, navy blue knickers and navy blue skirt and red jumpers and running pumps.

Breakfast, including porridge, was made in a large cauldron over a large open fire. We had to take out the dead wasps before we could eat it, we had treacle on it, then jam and bread. I remember we had tripe and onions done in milk some days, other days we had sausage. Tea was jam and bread and a bun.

We had six girls to look after, we went for walks or on the cliffs, the sands were very soft so we presumed they were quick sands. We found moles and dead rabbits – very exciting at our age.

We ate blackberries we found in the hedgerows.

The camp played rounders with the school from Silverdale, I played in the team. I was known as blondie because I was fair-haired.

Good memories.

Nellie Simpson nee Kemp

I was about eleven. It would be 1931. I remember some long paths. We went on the beach. We were all a bit rough in those days – tomboys. I liked anything like that. Going about, travelling about.

Mabel Brooksbank

Smiling Mrs Currer Briggs, 1935

OBITUARY 18 November, 1936

MRS. CURRER BRIGGS

Her Work for Women and Children

SEASIDE CAMP

Energy of Former Lady Mayoress of Leeds

"The Yorkshire Post" regrets to announce the death of Mrs. Currer Briggs, widow of the late Mr. Arthur Currer Briggs, J.P., which occurred last night at The Garth, King Lane, Leeds. She was in her 77th year.

By far the greater part of Mrs. Currer Briggs's life was given to philanthropic work, especially on behalf of women and children. She was a fine type of social worker, one who combined with sympathetic womanly interest, ability to deal with essentials in organisation, and energy to perform what heart and head prescribed.

Long before her position as Lady Mayoress in 1903-4 gave special opportunities for the exercise of her talents, she was actively engaged in benevolent work of one sort or another. As a member of the

Mrs. Currer Briggs

University News

OXFORD PROCTORS REPLY

Undergraduates and Armistice Service

The Proctors at Oxford, Mr. C. H. S. Fifoot

I gather it's a wonderful place now, but my story is an unhappy one.

I was born 19th September 1926 and I went to Silverdale Camp when I was eight. I had my ninth birthday during that dreadful two weeks. My dad took me to a school somewhere out of the town centre. When Dad left me, I was upset but didn't cry. I came from a large, poor family. A kind lady gave me a bath. (I'd just had one in the tub at home). She told me I had lovely feet. She then dressed me in a rough dark navy frock. She said, 'I'm sorry love there aren't any more check pinnies left to brighten it up'. She said, 'You have to wear the shoes they provide for you and there's only two left feet left for you'. She was nearly in tears. I was oblivious to this till I came to put them on and wore them the whole two weeks.

The couple who ran the place, wow! they didn't like kids as far as we could see. Breakfast was humble dripping and bread, put here and there on long tables. You dived in and got your share. Not me. I was too polite or too scared so I rarely got any.

One day I fell off the swing outside and bumped my head. I felt awful. I was dragged up from the floor and told I was all right. My friend later ran to tell them I wasn't, I was very sick. So what. I recovered. The Lord Mayor came whilst I was there and the man who ran the show was given sweets for us. When the Lord Mayor had gone the sweets were thrown up in the air. If you were quick you got some. I didn't.

My feet hurt terribly the whole time. When I came home I had lost weight. I had impetigo on my face. Our doctor at home was angry. He knew I'd been a

healthy, chubby, smiling kid, even though we were poor, no one at home wanted me to go on this holiday, but the do-gooders knew best.

I'm 77 years old. We survived the poverty. I've enjoyed my life and me and my lovely husband nearly 80 have had some lovely times together. Super holidays abroad. Good luck to you.

Ann Brown

The Babies' Room at the Camp was named the Helen Currer Briggs room. Mrs R M Currer Briggs and Mrs D H Currer Briggs, her daughters-in-law, kept the link between the family and the Association alive by coming onto the Committee. Also joining the Committee at that time were Mr Percy Smith, representing the Head Teachers' Association and Mr Bernard Mason.

Plumping up the children had been a source of pride for the Association for thirty odd years. For the past fourteen years children had gained an average of about three and a half pounds each during their holiday. In 1935 that gain dropped to less than three pounds. The difference in weight before and after the holiday became less marked after the widespread distribution of free milk in elementary schools.

The diet at the Camp also improved. Helen Briggs had long praised the benefits of good, cheap food, saying that mothers could learn from the Camp's example. She would have been pleased to see the introduction of 'raw fruit' at the Camp.

In 1937 Dr W H Waddington no longer needed to perform his fortnightly examination of children before they went to camp because this job was taken over by the Staff of the Medical Clinic of the Leeds Education Committee.

This procedure of medical examination lasted, in some form or other, until 1994.

During the Annual Civic Visit 1937, Lord Mayor, Tom Coombs, caused a bit of a stir in what would today be called his motivational address. He urged the boys to try and make something of their lives; to set themselves a definite goal, and aim high. He offered three prizes of ten shillings each for the best essays on the boys' visit to the camp. Thirty-one essayists rose to the challenge and provided a Boy's Eye View of Camp life. The winners were Eric Steel, Harold Sheffield and James Burns.

I arrived at Silverdale and walked to the Camp. When I got there I thought it looked a very dumb place, but at last I got to like it. There is some very good views around and you can see Morecambe Bay in the distance. I like this place and the food is very plain even so it is good. After breakfast it is very pleasant and we are always in the wood. There is a little wood but it is out of bounds so no one is allowed out of bounds or they will be sent back to Leeds immediately.

There are two maids one is called May and the other one Clara. Clara took us and Mrs. Bucknall to the top of a cliff and we saw one of the best sights of England. It is very hot here and we generally get very tired near bedtime. The tide comes very high up in the afternoon.

Last Saturday the Lord Mayor and Lady Mayoress came to see us and we didn't half enjoy ourselves at least I did. We went into a room and the Chairwomen and Chairman Dr. Waere had a talk to us and a lot more people. Then he introduced the Lord Mayor to us and we all clapped.

The Lord Mayor said that he would give a prize to the three best essays of ten shillings. The essay had to be about Camp.

Then Mr. Riley a man who writes books stood up and spoke a few words.

After that Dr. Waere stood up and said, 'Now I will ask Peter Evans to present the Lady Mayoress with a bunch of delightful flowers.'

Serving fish and potatoes

'I will now ask my Lady Mayoress to stand up and say a few words,' he said.

And she did but not much because the Lord Mayor had spoken for her.

After two more men had spoke we walked out each receiving two bars of chocolate and a bag of sweets.

Then we had our photos taken and the Lord Mayor stood and James Burns and I were the only two taken in that photo the photographs were in the Leeds Mercury.

There was nothing else exciting that week but this week we went swimming in the sea and the water tasted just like crab and salmon.

The cricket match was cancelled because the village did not turn up.

There is a hospital and it is for them who have diseases at all. While we have been here a boy called Burns has been taken to Lancashire (Lancaster) Hospital with newmonia. Another one has hurt his eye with a cork ball, and another has stuck a nail in his wrist.

Now I think I will have to close and I think this is my very best holiday I've ever had.

Harold Sheffield

SILVERDALE *a magical name, bringing back memories of happy childhood days before the war. We were taken to the Children's holiday camp beside the sea. The weather was glorious. My friend and I wandered to the cliff top, laying on our tummies relaxing in the hot weather watching butterflies and beautiful harebells. Forgetting all about time we never heard the dinner gong, until someone came to call us. Potatoes with the skin on, but tasty just the same. Punishment for being late was to be sent out into the garden to pick fruit for tea. This was really a pleasure as the lovely scents and luscious red fruit made it memorable. Another day was spent making a big den out of bracken and fern. Entwining them to make a roof. We were then told of a trip the following day to the Pepper Pot. We were in crocodile formation and so happy, I was singing and a lady stopped and gave me half- a-crown, which was duly taken towards funds. We were instructed to walk three times round the Pepper Pot and make a wish. I wished for a doll. That night we were so excited we were having a good laugh in the dormitory. We were told to be quiet and go to sleep. The trouble was, when I had a giggling fit, I couldn't stop, so was sent to stand in the window bay till I was quiet. This was no punishment either, for standing there was looking at fairy-land to me. All the lights of Morecambe Bay were twinkling and smiling at me, and I could have stayed there all night. All too soon, it was time to go home, but the treat didn't stop there. While I had been away, my Aunt Millie in Scotland had sent a parcel to us, and guess what had been sent to me, - a doll. Who says wishes aren't granted! Thank you for lovely memories.*

Milly A Rodgers

Roy Dixon lives in Morecambe. He moved there because his brother John told him of the beauty of Morecambe Bay, which he remembered from his holiday as a lad at Silverdale. John Dixon, who died in 1994, wrote a poem that Roy has carried in his wallet for years.

It was over 50 years ago when I was just a lad

My father didn't have a job and times were very bad.

They called my name out at school, I didn't have much say.

The teacher said, You lucky lad you're off to Morecambe Bay.

That night my mother scrubbed me well she wouldn't have no shame

But when I got to a place in Leeds they scrubbed me once again.

So shining clean but underfed and all dressed up the same, in long black cloaks all lined in red we went to catch a train.

It must have been a sorry sight to see those little boys marching off to they know not what so they didn't make much noise.

So spare a thought for those tiny tots they may be looking pale

But they're on their way for a holiday to a place called Silverdale.

John Dixon

I was born at 42 Bayswater Street in a back-to-back terrace house having a shared toilet block some yards down the street. We had an attic and a cellar but only one bedroom and no bathroom.

I went to school initially to Roundhay Road elementary, plus St Aidan's Sunday School. It was 1938 when Rowland my elder brother and I were told/selected to go on the trip to Silverdale. I was seven and Rowland nine. I struggled with the memory a bit, and unfortunately my brother who went with me, and all the rest of my family, have passed on so I had no one to check things with, but thinking about it brought back some details. I think we went on a Sammy Ledgard coach, of the famous Leeds bus company.

I remember lots of walking, through woods and on the beach and some lessons were carried on. One day a beach group were caught, or chased by the swift incoming tide, and as we ran for the cliff paths out, one lad stepped into one of many deep pools and yelled out as he put his foot on a big nail. It was huge and he screamed a lot as we were forced to carry him the final yards to safety and back to camp. Sorry, I cannot remember his name.

Overall, the stay was hugely enjoyable I recall. I remember being lost on our return to Leeds but got home by following the tramlines up Roundhay Road to the Bayswaters.

Two years later, and I was away with my gas mask as an Evacuee to Copmanthorpe. But that as they say, was quite another story.

Douglas Dale

continued.
YEP. 22/7/45

Leeds children's friend dies at 88

Evening Post Reporter

MR. TOM WILSON, first superintendent of Leeds Children's Holiday Camp at Silverdale, Morecambe, from its opening in 1904 till 1936, has died, aged 88.

He was known to thousands of Leeds people who spent a holiday at the camp as children.

About 20,000 children had been in his care at Silverdale during his 32 years in charge of the camp. The grandparents and parents of some of the children attending the camp today were themselves campers when Mr. Wilson was there.

When the camp was first established in 1904 at Hest Bank, further along the Morecambe Bay coast, it was experimental, and much of the credit for its subsequent success was due to Mr. Wilson.

Girls waiting to go to camp

34

THE SECOND WORLD WAR

In September 1938, British Prime Minister Chamberlain, French Prime Minister Daldier, Italian Prime Minister Mussolini and German Chancellor Hitler met in Munich. They signed the Munich Agreement which allowed Germany to take over the Sudetan area of Czechoslovakia. During that month, when it looked as if there was a strong possibility of war breaking out, the Committee offered the Camp to the Lord Mayor 'for any purpose connected with Leeds children, on terms the best possible within the Constitution of the Association'. The Lord Mayor acknowledged the proposal, but the Camp was not needed. In December 1938, the Committee expressed a willingness to take refugees from Germany or Czechoslovakia, but again it was not needed.

James Bucknall, Camp Superintendent, was a Naval Reservist, but on the third list for call up. (In the event, he was not called up for war service.) He put in place a plan to evacuate the children, without alarming them, to a position at the foot of the cliffs if hostile aircraft were spotted in the area. Wellington boots and waterproofs were to be provided and there was the question of having a supply of gas masks, so that the children would not have to carry them from Leeds individually.

Germany invaded Poland. On September 3rd, 1939, Britain and France declared war on Germany. Sixty-seven children were at the Camp when war was declared. The School Medical Officer advised that they be brought back to Leeds, and that no more should be sent because of the difficulties of food and transport.

There were prolonged discussions about whether Westmorland County Council would take over the Camp for evacuee children from Newcastle and South Shields. Meanwhile, many evacuees and their parents voted with their feet against evacuation. From all directions, children had returned to their homes - a 'homeward flood', during the time when not much seemed to be happening – the period known as 'the phoney war'. The Ministry of Health decided not to go along with Westmorland County Council's proposal to evacuate children to Silverdale.

Dr Algernon Wear had taken on the chairmanship of the Association after Helen Briggs' death. He was one of the four people who, back in 1903, took the first steps towards creating the Association. He and others were mindful that during the last war the Camp had stayed open for the children. They were keen to do so again if the difficulties over food and transport could be overcome.

Perhaps another war was the last straw for the now elderly Miss Richardson. She had worked tirelessly as Enquiry Agent and Secretary for over thirty five years. During the First World War she visited the homes of all the boys from across Leeds who had joined the services and gone to fight. Many did not return, or came home in a pitiful condition. 1938 was her last year as Organising Secretary. She retired in 1939 but stayed on in a voluntary capacity as Consulting Secretary, until her death in 1945. Helen Briggs had received richly deserved honours, a tablet carved with her name, and a room named after her. Others who had generously donated money had plaques, rooms or beds named in their memory. Miss Richardson received no lasting memorial. Many Committee Members and Subscribers left generous legacies to the Association. My guess is that Miss Richardson had nothing to leave. She gave all she had to give – herself, her common sense, her compassion and her shoe leather.

The old guard were dying – and they stayed in post until they died. After his long service to the Association, Dr Algernon Wear died in 1941. In the Annual Reports the necessarily brief accounts of the demise of committee members give an insight into the nature of their work, and sometimes their personalities. Mrs Abbott of the Ladies Auxiliary Committee was a worker whose cheerful kindliness would be greatly missed at the Tuesday afternoon sewing sessions where the children's clothes were mended, after being dry-cleaned free of charge by Crockatts.

The Committee and Mr and Mrs Bucknall did keep the Camp open during the Second World War, in spite of shortage of staff and food rationing. Plenty of families had low incomes, entitling them to a holiday for their children. Particular consideration was given where one or more family member was away at war and the mother could not work because of the needs of younger children.

Not only did the Camp stay open, but the Committee came up with new ideas. Mr Snape, News Editor of the Yorkshire Post, joined the Committee. Years later, Mr Snape's daughter, Barbara Snape, left a generous bequest to the Association.

The links with the University were strengthened when Mrs Grist was elected after Professor E O James relinquished membership.

The former Treasurer, Mr Fryer, had introduced a covenant scheme of subscription so that the Association could reclaim tax. Such covenants are now known as Gift Aid. The new Treasurer, Mr Popplewell, opened a Building Fund to provide permanent buildings at Silverdale. It had the ambitious aim of reaching £10,000.

The General Committee are greatly obliged to Miss. Muriel Levy (Auntie Muriel of the B.B.C.) for permission to reprint her 1943 broadcast poem, which very felicitously expresses what must have been felt by many of the 24,488 children who have been to the Camp since 1904.
It is as follows:

TOWN AND COUNTRY CHILD.
I never knew that far from town
With all its dirt and noise,
Were fields and trees and lovely spots
For little girls and boys.
The only birds I've ever seen
Are sparrows in the street;
I never knew that country birds
Could sing so high and sweet,
I've never seen a pig before
Except in city shops,
And then it's only bacon, or
A pound of nice pork chops.
I've only seen a tired horse
That trudges up the road,
But now I've seen one in a field
Without its heavy load.
I never knew the sun was warm
I've always hated rain;
But I've been in a country shower
And life is sweet again!

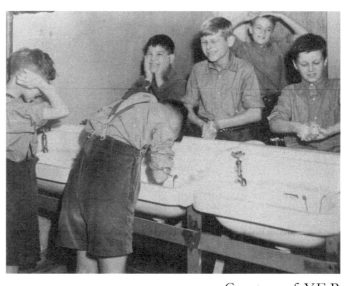

Courtesy of Y.E.P.

Mr Popplewell proved right to set an ambitious target for the re-building of the camp. Alderman Rowland Winn, who as Mayor had paid for one hundred children to go on holiday, now gave £10,000 to the fund. It was in the form of an interest free loan to government, due to be paid back at the end of the war.

In 1938 the Camp had, 'at long last, secured an ample, piped water supply from the adjacent Local Authority'. Now, in 1943, Architect Mr G Alan Burnett drew up a scheme for the construction of a modern holiday camp, designed to accommodate larger numbers of children – though the running costs would be higher. The Architect was keen to create the kind of structure that would avoid an institutionalised atmosphere.

The opening of the Camp had been postponed for a fortnight in 1944 because of the lack of domestic help. The number of children sent in each 'batch' was reduced to 30. Students from Bingley Training College helped during their vacation, going to the Camp in pairs for three successive fortnights. Mrs Bucknall's sisters also helped throughout the season. This allowed the number to be increased to 40. But the Medical Officers of the Education Committee, who had charge of examining children before their departure for the Camp, turned down a great number of the girls so that they remained at 30, and only the number of boys was increased.

One girl who was turned down remembers the experience.

I'm seventy now. I remember going, it would be the early 1940s, and being examined and they looked in your hair and everything. I was very thin and poorly, at the clinic every week, and used to get sties. I would have been about seven. We were very poor, living on Spring Street. Anyhow, the camp turned me down. We had a letter and I think they must have turned me down because I was poorly.

Joyce Leach (nee Greenwood)

Courtesy of Y.E.P.

Writing in 2004, Alan Tomlinson, Chairman of the Silverdale local Committee, looks back to the days of the Second World War, and the Camp's historic link with HMS Ark Royal.

The Camp's links with the Ark Royal the Aircraft Carrier go back some 65 years to the Second World War. In 1940, England was fighting for her life. Germany occupied all Europe, apart from Britain. One of the important bastions that stood between our country and Germany was HMS Ark Royal. In 1940 she sailed off Norway where she had badly damaged a German Battleship. In a later battle, the German Bismarck sank our own Battleship The Hood with a large loss of life. Churchill sent out the message, 'Sink the Bismarck'. A Swordfish from the Ark Royal found the Bismarck and caused damage to its rudder, making it helpless. Shortly afterwards the Bismarck was sunk. Unfortunately six months later the Ark Royal was sunk by a torpedo off Gibraltar. Thankfully only one seaman was lost and all the crew were saved. The City of Leeds then contributed to purchase a new Ark Royal and from that point onwards the Officers and Men of the Ark Royal wanted to show gratitude to the City and in particular they found friendship with the Leeds Children's Holiday Home. During the past fifteen years, Seamen and Officers from the present Ark Royal have visited and stayed at the Camp and enjoyed hospitality and friendship with us. As a special gesture, the Captain of the Ark Royal invited the Warden, David Johnston and Debbie the matron to spend two nights on the Ark Royal which we consider was a real honour as it is a very rare event indeed for civilians to be invited in this way. The invitation was well deserved because David was an excellent organiser and a very popular Warden, strong, kind and considerate. He had a commanding voice and was very well respected by both staff and children.

Alan Tomlinson

Singing with Leeds Amateur Operatic Society

THE WELFARE STATE

Prime Minister Harold Macmillan became well-known for his 1957 'never had it so good' comment: 'Let's be frank about it; most of our people have never had it so good'.

1957 or 1958

Like most things, that's probably debatable. The post-war period did see many improvements for children. Nursery school children, or infants as we were called, formed a circle for our spoonfuls of cod liver oil and orange juice. Everyone got free school milk. In winter, milk crates were place in front of the classroom fire to warm. I hated milk. The teacher tried to persuade me to drink, by pouring it into a china cup and keeping me back at playtime. I am still grateful to Infant Joseph Barnes of St Charles's School. Day after day, he gallantly fetched my coat from the cloakroom and polished off my untouched milk so that we could go out to play. Undernourished kids went on receiving malt throughout their school days, much to the envy of those of us who liked malt but didn't qualify. 'I'd like malt,' I would say. 'I'm small.'

No one told me I was small because I wouldn't drink my milk, but that I was small because my parents were small. The malt children needed nourishment.

My own feeling about those never-had-it-so-good days is a profound conviction that fewer girls had head lice than ever before, or ever since.

Nurses went into schools, examined heads and sent the child home with a note to buy *Derbac* and a nit comb.

Head lice had been a problem at the camp from the earliest days. Helen Briggs once proposed that girls have their hair cut before going to the camp. Superintendent Tom Wilson thought it would be a better idea if girls with short hair be given preference over long-haired girls, and that it should say that, on the application form. It did.

Mrs Dibb, writing to the Yorkshire Evening Post in 1997, remembered going to the Camp in 1947. Every girl had to have pigtails, no matter how short her hair. She also remembered the badge on the blazer with its big red letters LPCHC, which told them that the coat belonged to the Leeds Poor Children's Holiday Camp.

Nits or no nits, throughout the never-had-it-so-good period, teachers, head teachers, the NSPCC, the Discharged Prisoners' Aid Society and hospital almoners still referred lots of children for free holidays. Despite the welfare state, it could take just one misfortune to tip a family into economic trouble.

A family of seven children who had lost their mother and whose father was in hospital were temporarily 'adopted' by neighbours, one of whom had eight children. All fifteen children found their way to Silverdale.

I spent two holidays there. In 1946 I went off alone. In 1947 I went with my sister. One of the things I remember is Lizzie Lord being made to crawl under the bungalow to 'rescue' three kittens. She was chosen because she was the skinniest girl there. When we peeled the potatoes woe betide us if we took too much potato with the peel because we found it mashed up with the spuds. Girls who had been to camp before, warned us to sleep with our knickers under the pillow. If any girl broke her knicker elastic it was rumoured that she would look for a better pair when the rest of us were asleep. I also remember the walks. We went onto the beach and were warned about the quicksand. The best thing that I remember is that on both occasions it didn't rain for the whole two weeks. We all came home as brown as berries.

Iris Crow
(on BBC Look North)

I remember as if it were yesterday. My father was out of work and it all started at Blenheim CP School on Blackman Lane. At the school we all had to get bathed then changed into the clothes provided for us – brown corduroy trousers, socks with red and grey hoops, navy blue jersey with arm bands and a black shoulder cape like the police used to wear.

After all this we were marched down to the train station.

On the train journey there, one of the lads in our compartment was playing around and accidentally got his cap caught in the communication cord and stopped the train.

So we had to report to the head man as soon as we arrived at the camp and all in all we got off to a bad start.

The camp was situated on top of a cliff and the accommodation was billets like we had in the army.

The chap in charge was called Mr Bucknall and he was very strict.

In the dining room you all had to sit up straight and no noise, then after meals you all mucked in to clean all the pots and pans.

One day out on a walk an old lady gave me two and sixpence, which was a lot of money in 1947.

Later on I found out that all money given to us on walks had to go into the poor box which was on a shelf in the dining room.

It's the only holiday camp I've been to where we never saw the sea. The tide went out on a morning before we got up and came in at night when we were in bed. For all this I wouldn't have missed it for the world.

L Dickinson, letter to YEP

In 1947 I was hoping to go to the school camp near Ilkley but it would have cost my family five shillings to send me. My father was unemployed and my mother was bringing up six children, all at school.

An uncle offered the money but unfortunately the pay-camp was full by then. He approached the Leeds Poor Children's Holiday Camp and somehow I was given a place for the summer. This was my first holiday ever.

My mum took me down to the offices which were upstairs in Calverley Street, Leeds, and with approximately 35 other boys we were kitted out with khaki shorts and navy blue sweaters, with red rings round the arms. Our own clothes were put in the office for two weeks or taken home to await our return.

We set off by bus and I think it was one of Sammy Ledgard's. It was a long journey because we did not have motorways in those days. The camp was run like a military camp, very efficient and over-disciplined by Mr Bucknall and his wife.

They had a daughter, Rose, who also helped out. I will always remember the dripping sandwiches and the cocoa at supper time.

I remember the five-mile walks round country lanes and across the bay. I collected small crabs, shells, and crab apples.

I remember a party of us being late back for lunch after being at the beach. We had been out of bounds and one bright lad picked a bunch of bluebells and said they were for Rose. It got us off the hook slightly but the supper amounts were reduced.

Finally I sent a postcard to my mum asking her to bring a suitcase – borrowed – from neighbours – to accommodate the crabs, shells, crab apples etc. Needless to say the crabs were dead, shells broken, and the apples uneatable. Perhaps I should have fed the crabs with them.

I have never had a crab of any sort since.

Colin Broadbent, letter to YEP

I attended the camp just after the War, about 1947-1950. I remember receiving a set of clothes at Great George Street. Coming from a large family, this alone I found most rewarding.

During my stay I became friends with one of the dinner ladies. We corresponded for several years. I often think of her and wonder if she is okay. I did receive a photo from her, following her marriage.

The most vivid impression that has stayed with me following my visits to Silverdale is standing at the main entrance and reading, several times: Leeds Poor Children's Holiday Camp.

I am eternally grateful to the people of Leeds who through their sponsorship gave children such as myself a most rewarding and enjoyable holiday.

Stanley Thompson

Swimming lesson, 1957

The old kitchen

I remember going to Silverdale in the late 50s twice. My memory of the camp is the outdoor swimming pool. My biggest memory is that I had an accident and fell out of a tree and ended up in Morecambe hospital. We were only allowed to take half a crown spending money. This had to last the two weeks.

Ray Emmerson,
courtesy
of BBC Look North

I was a Silverdale child, attending in 1950-1953, aged 8 to 11. I remember buses left Great George Street in Leeds. The bus journey took so long it seemed the other side of the world.

On arrival we were allocated to the Red or the Blue dormitory and they played against each other at football and cricket.

The Camp Master was Mr Bucknall, a terribly strict disciplinarian, but also very fair.

We could take only a maximum of £1 spending money which was held by the camp. They had a camp tuck shop which operated at 6pm for one hour and we were allowed to spend a maximum of one shilling a day, thereby making sure the money lasted for the full fortnight.

We had to take turns on duties which included peeling potatoes, washing pots and keeping the site tidy. The fresh air usually tired us out and lights out was nine o'clock.

Days were organised to Morecambe Bay (where we had a paddle) and to Bowness to see the boats on Lake Winderemere.

One year we stayed the fortnight in a big house in Bowness whilst repairs were carried out at Silverdale.

The weather was usually good, but if poor we could stay indoors and play table tennis and plenty of board games.

We were given two sets of clothing, one for each week and they had to last, unless there was an emergency, when there was a large stock of spares. You were lucky if you got something to fit perfectly.

They were really wonderful days and it was with great sadness when the day arrived to go back home to Leeds.

I have no recollection of any names of boys who were there except for John Smith, from Middleton, who was there at the same time as me two years running.

Wonderful days indeed!

Robert Stone

I went to Silverdale around 1957 or 1958. I was about six years old at the time. I remember the walks in the woods. I think I remember a little castle nearby. We went to church on a Sunday, they dressed us all up. They gave you coppers to put in the box after the service.

Looking at the footage on Look North tonight, I remember the outdoor pool so clearly. I have so many memories of that place. We had a recreation room where we played games. We also played football and went swimming. We slept in corridors with beds in long rows. It would be wonderful to hear of people who went to Silverdale at the same time as myself.

G. Wortley, Leeds,
courtesy
of BBC Look North

Both my younger sister and I would natter my mum constantly as to when we would be going on our holidays as this was a novelty to us, because we had heard so much about it from our older brothers and sisters and couldn't wait to go on our first holiday – for two weeks, wow!

I had a new navy blazer given. It had all the buttons and was very smart, plus it was warm and the best thing was nobody had worn it before me because when you came from a large family everything was passed down numerous times.

The lovely big house in Bowness was just on a bend. It had a front wooden porch. A narrow hallway to the left was where we hung our coats. I didn't want to leave mine. We met Mr and Mrs Bucknall, whom I thought were very old.

Then we went up this double staircase and were shown our bedrooms. I think we had six single beds. This was bliss, not having to share a bed with anyone else. The wind would howl down the chimney and one of the older girls would frighten us by saying it was ghosts. We would end up in tears and Mr Bucknall would come in and tell them off.

I remember going for a walk through this field full of cows and the gate seemed miles away and Mr Bucknall would say, 'Keep in line. They won't hurt you.' Famous last words. They were huge.

We took the ferry to an island on Lake Windermere, it was full of daffodils. We had a picnic and tiring ourselves out we didn't think of the time. We had to walk back dead tired. But you could hear Mr Bucknall saying, 'Keep going. Not far now!' Huh!

The next year we stayed in the new, modern building at Silverdale. The dorms held lots of beds. It was a mad dash to get next to the friends you'd made on the coach. But not for long as Mrs Bucknall would soon change girls about if she thought they would upset the rest.

We had a huge lounge where you could read or play board games. It was called the quiet room but was not quiet for long as someone would soon accuse someone else of cheating.

My sister and I with another girl were told to go with a tin bath into a nearby field and collect cow pats for Mr Bucknall's little garden to the left of the front door. It took us ages to carry it back as we weren't that big. We used to have a race around the building if it had been cold, to warm us up. But I did win and I received a huge apple.

I vaguely remember jam and bread with cocoa for supper and the meals must have been lovely because I didn't leave any.

I look back on these times with fond memories and especially of Mr and Mrs Bucknall, him in his tweed jacket, walking stick and a ruddy face. They were really kind.

I enjoyed myself and would look forward to it. It was not a stigma to go because everyone was in the same position.

Elaine Hartley

Silverdale was gorgeous.
I was about eight years old and I remember the trips went from Great George Street.
When we arrived, we'd get a postcard to send home. We went out on long walks.
Somebody used to bring apples from an orchard and on Sundays we all got an apple.
One girl sang 'Swing Low Sweet Chariot'.
It is something I will never ever forget.

Christine Pinkney,
courtesy of BBC Radio Leeds

'The Wizard of Oz' starts in black and white and bursts into glorious technicolour when Dorothy reaches Oz. The cover of the Leeds Poor Children's Holiday Camp Association's Annual Report for 1950 burst into red, white and blue – and stayed red, white and blue until 1953. There were reasons to be cheerful.

1949 had been wonderfully fine, sunny year. In May, Leeds Amateurs staged Wild Violets and donated £1,500 to the camp. The Workpeople's Hospital Fund added £5,000 to the building fund. The Superintendent's annual report said that it was the best season for many years, with the children in good health, sports on Whit Monday, and lots of gifts brought to the Camp from Silverdale and Leeds friends.

The old camp had served its purpose. It was demolished. Work on Mr G Alan Burnett's superb art deco design modern holiday camp building was about to begin.

Rowland Winn lays the foundation stone

Twenty-five holidaying Leeds girls came across for the day from their temporary accommodation at Langrigg House, Bowness, Windermere. They were a smaller party than usual because of reduced cooking facilities at Langrigg House. Two seasons were spent at Bowness, taking ferry or steamer trips on the lake, climbing Wansdale Pike or Orrest Head and visiting

My parents took over at the camp in 1936 and were wardens for twenty years. I would have been about fourteen then and was attending the College of Commerce in Leeds, staying with an aunt for a year or so. Later I went to night school in Lancaster. I got a job in Milnthorpe, about five miles from Silverdale. There wasn't any public transport to Milnthorpe. For nearly thirteen years, in all weathers, I cycled ten miles a day.

There were about 56 children and so my parents had to be strict disciplinarians. Father used to take them for long walks in a crocodile. Children went on the beach, but not on their own. It was safer then than it is now, due to changes in the tide. I played rounders and cricket with the children which I enjoyed, being on the sporty side myself.

We were light years away from Leeds. There wasn't any street lighting; water had to be gathered in tanks around the building. Electricity was generated and the old camp was army huts for the children. Accommodation was in a big dormitory. We had minute bedrooms – I had one and my parents had another.

It was hard work but my parents enjoyed it. My mother cooked on a big black range with two ovens on either side. How she used to cook for fifty six or sixty children every day I just don't know. We had no fridge. All through the summer it was a continuous seven day a week job for them.

Mother and father were there when it was decided to pull down the old building. They were asked to try and find alternative accommodation. They found a place at Bowness-on-Windermere, a former nursing home called Langrigg.

Mary Brand

Stock Ghyll Waterfall. Both girls and boys enjoyed fishing. Using only string and bent pins, two boys caught four perch.

The wet summer of 1951 caused delays in constructing the new building. The labour shortage in the building trade was felt in urban areas and much more so on the remote, country site. Severe frosts in the winter of 1951-52 delayed finishing outside, and indoor plastering. Building costs rose sharply during 1951.

Generous donors included a further £5,000 from Rowland Winn, making £15,000 in all. Leeds and District Workpeople's Hospital Fund gave £1,000 for the Building Fund plus £250 for general maintenance and holidays. Leeds District Union of Golf Clubs and Leeds Golfers' Committee donated the proceeds of their Golf Ball, Competition and Cabaret. Yorkshire Automobile Club gave £1,200.

On Thursday, 24 April 1952, the 'magnificent new building' was opened by Mr Rowland Winn, MBE, JP, and was ready to receive children by the middle of July. It boasted spacious, airy rooms – a play room large enough for indoor cricket, concerts, hopscotch, skipping and all the games that are usually considered 'outdoor games.' The games room had two table tennis boards and several small tables for board games. The television room was also used for showing films. The eight acres of grounds, when completed, provided pitches for cricket, football, netball and rounders as well as woodlands to explore.

James Bucknall's Superintendent's Report conveys the atmosphere of that first season in the new building.

"There was great excitement on July 18th, 1952, when the first party of children arrived at the Home for their holiday. They were delighted with all they saw and thoroughly enjoyed their fortnight, as did each succeeding party. The children showed their appreciation for all that was done for them. Owing to improved cooking facilities we were able to provide more varied meals. The cinema projector proved its worth, and we had an excellent supply of films. The new projection room is a great asset. The Sunday School services were resumed with the help of. Mrs. Burrow and Mrs. Johnson, who came every Sunday. We are most grateful to them.

The three students from Bingley Training College, who each stayed two weeks with the children were a great help and we were sorry when their visits ended. With the help of Mr. W. Riley, an Open, Day was held in August for local residents and visitors. This proved a great success, for more than two hundred people visited the home and expressed their admiration. The Silverdale Committee, the staff, and the students showed the visitors round, afterwards serving tea. The children also much enjoyed the day when the Leeds and District Workpeople's Hospital Fund Committee came to see the home towards which they had contributed so generously, as well as presenting furniture. They gave the children fruit, sweets, books and games, and expressed their pleasure when the girls, who had been trained by the Bingley students and Sunday School leaders, sang to them."

LAOS members by the pool paid for from the proceeds of *Careless Rapture*

Coronation Day 2nd June, 1953, was celebrated with a sports meeting in the afternoon, tea, a decorated cake and a film show. Each child received a decorated mug.

During the Association's Jubilee Year, 1954, 269 boys and 283 girls spent a fortnight at the new Holiday Home. Since 1904, a total of 29,518 children had experienced a fortnight's free holiday at the seaside. To their £1,000 donated from the proceeds of 'Annie Get Your Gun', Leeds Amateur Operatic Society added the proceeds of their production of 'Careless Rapture' and paid for the pool where I would learn to swim. It was opened by Robert Barr, President of the Leeds Amateur Operatic Society on 22nd May 1955. Robert Barr of Wallace Arnold Tours ('every mile a magnificent mile') provided coaches to take children to and from the camp.

In 1955 there was an outbreak of measles and scarlet fever – the first epidemic for fifteen years. Some girls were sent to the nearest isolation hospital and the home was closed for a week for fumigation.

Mr and Mrs Bucknall retired after twenty years, to take up less arduous work.

In one of the coldest wettest summers for decades, enter Mr and Mrs Ernest Farrar and Miss Teresa Farrar. If it sounds like a game of Happy Families, well that's what it felt like to me. I was not alone. The reports of the following eight years contain children's letters of warm appreciation.

Ernest Farrar's Report, 1957

The children enjoyed to the full the swimming pool, round-about, swings, cricket, football. netball, rounders, Indians and Cowboys. Both girls and boys enjoyed the opportunity of climbing the trees. Every day we went for long walks, visiting all the beauty spots in and around Silverdale. Every evening the children watched Children's Hour on T.V. During the cold and wet days the games room, which included two full sized Table Tennis tables, was a great boon. Inter-games with the village school caused great excitement. Birthday parties were an enormous success, and the idea of organising their own concerts was a big thrill for the boys and girls. One party of girls arranged three pantomimes: "Jack and the Beanstalk", "Cinderella", and "Sleeping Beauty", and for the latter they made their own costumes of crepe paper.

Many will wonder what we do with ourselves during the winter; I can assure you there is plenty to do. Our building is enormous and the interior requires spring cleaning, the swimming pool needs cleaning out and swings and round-about overhauling. There is mending to be done, the building to be aired and tidied, and the grounds kept in proper order."

Dear Mr. & Mrs. Farrar, I would like to thank you both for giving my son Stephen a nice holiday. It is the first one he has ever had as my husband has had a lot of illness in the past few years, and a few months ago he had to retire from work owing to illness and his age, so you can guess it was a godsend for us that Stephen could have his holiday as he has talked about one for a long time. Anyway, once again we thank you.

(A Mother).

Dear Mr. & Mrs. Farrar, staff and Lassie (Mr. Farrar's dog).

Just a few lines in which to thank you for a wonderful and successful holiday in Silverdale and to thank you for the great and active part you have played in helping children of Leeds to a welcome and happy holiday. While I am writing this short letter I am almost crying to think how we got along together and enjoyed the scenery and joyful times we had together. When I leave school I will come and see you. I hope you are a success and the children are good and helpful to you as you deserve it very much. I send all my love and thanks.

June (aged 13)

Owing to the lovely weather most of the days were spent out of doors, the favourite attraction being the swimming pool which was in full use until the end of the season. More than fifty children were taught to swim correctly and many more taught themselves to do the free style splash and splash crawl. One day the Headmaster of Osmandthorpe School paid us a surprise visit and two of his scholars greeted him with, "We can swim now, sir." He turned to me to offer a word of praise, but my satisfaction was short lived when I saw their free for all crawl. No wonder we had a water shortage.

The children visited many places of interest and the walks were enjoyed by all with the exception of the minority who expected to see a tram or a bus at every turn of the road.

In addition to games in the Camp grounds the children explored caves, romped over the salt marshes, jumped the dykes, and the things they imagined they saw would make David Attenborough green with envy. Many treasures, fish, crabs, winkles and shrimps were sought and found and what fisherman's tales were told on returning to Camp, tired, but happy.

Ernest Farrar's 1960 Report

> Dear Sir,
> We thank you for the lovely holiday and the kind attention we received when me and my brother was there. My Dad once came when he was a boy. He said he wished he could go again because I told him it was not the same building and there is a swimming pool.
> Love to all,
> David and Bernard.

> *Dear Mr. Farrar,*
> *Thank you very much for the good holiday you gave us. On the bus we all said hip, hip, hurray to Mr. Farrar and I said the boys were a little bit late in saying it. I liked my job in the dining room and I hope I will be able to do it again some day. I hope I am first to write to you so you can read my letter first. When I got home I played Conkers with the ones you gave me. Hope you pass by here: and drop in to see us. Well goodbye for now,*
> *Yours truly, John, Number 37 locker - Dining room boy.*

> *Dear Mr. & Mrs. Farrar,*
> *Just a few lines to thank you very much for my Granddaughter's holiday also the nice card for her birthday which was more than her Dad sent her. She keeps telling me bits and I think you do a wonderful job to keep all those youngsters entertained. I hope you have the ability to carry on the good work for a long time. I think Gillian looks much better. Thanking you both once again.*
> *Grandma.*

Supervising the swimming

1960 saw a record number of children visit the holiday camp, despite a wretched summer. Seven parties of boys numbering 331 and six parties of girls 300 – total 631, brought the total to 33,175 since the Association was founded.

Yvonne Warburton first started work with the Farrars in the National Children's Home, Bramhope. Yvonne worked at Silverdale for a year, but it did not provide a career structure. She went on to run a children's home herself, but remembers her time at Silverdale.

When the children arrived in the coach, weary and travel sick, they looked out over the salt-marsh with a shiny ribbon of water on the horizon and said "Miss, we'erst t' sea?", then looked round at the fields and trees and said "we' erst shops?"

On the first evening we washed all their hair with Derbac soap, for obvious reasons, and at that time all the boys had Tommy Steel crew cuts. After washing 25 Crew cuts with black soap I was covered in black spots!!!

Silverdale is a lovely place, and we could take the children on walks every day and find something different to visit each time - the Pepperpot, the Woodwell, the Fairy Ring, Jenny Brown's point, Arnside Knott, White Bay, the Smuggler's Cave and of course, the ruined Arnside Tower, where one considerate group of boys said to me "you sit here Miss and have a rest while we play goodies and baddies." I well remember taking a new group of boys to the Pepperpot, and we had to go through a very narrow stone stile. I have always been rather a large lady, and all these little boys went through first and turned and waited for me - not saying a word, but obviously anticipating that I would get stuck - I didn't!!!

It was an ideal place for children, particularly boys. There was a plantation of small trees in the grounds, and at dinner-time you could go out to call them in and there would not be a boy in sight. As soon as you blew the whistle, they all came dropping down out of the trees.

I was there when we had the outbreak of Asian 'Flu. We had heard the epidemic had reached Leeds, and when the next batch of boys arrived, one got off the 'bus saying "I think I've got Asian 'Flu." We very cleverly put him in the sick room and thought that was that. During the next two weeks we had 38 children and two staff poorly. Every mealtime we had to count afresh how many were in bed.

We had very few behaviour problems - the threat that their Headteachers (who had recommended them to come) would be told that they had let their school down, was usually enough to settle them down. Homesickness usually passed off within a day or two.

I would like to pay tribute to the work of Mr & Mrs Farrar. Their whole heart and soul was in the work. During the season they never had a day off together. Mrs Farrar's day off started after she had made the breakfasts, and she was back on duty after teatime. We all worked very hard for £5 a week plus our keep, but we enjoyed it and I have a lot of happy memories.

Yvonne Warburton

It was 1959 when I saw this advertisement in the Evening Post:

Staff needed for Leeds Children's Holiday Camp at Silverdale, Easter to October.

I always wanted to look after children but when I had applied for positions before and told them I had asthma they would say, 'Come back next year'.

I thought I would never be able to do the job I wanted. Since I was a small girl I looked after children playing out in the street. My dream was to look after children in a Children's Home.

I went to Great George Street office for an interview. I didn't tell them about my asthma. I was thrilled to be accepted.

When the time came to go to Silverdale, I was very nervous as I had not lived away from home on my own before.

The morning I set off it was snowing in Leeds so I got all dressed up in a raincoat and Wellingtons. When I arrived at Carnforth, the sun was shining, it was a beautiful day.

Another girl got off the same train. Mr Farrar picked us up at the station and took us to Silverdale.

I loved the place as soon as we went through the big gate. I had only seen photographs before. We were introduced to Ann, who lived locally, at Warton, and to Mrs Farrar. They had prepared a meal for us. After this we were taken on a grand tour of the building.

There were twenty beds in each dormitory with drawer units down the middle. The beds had red blankets, white pillowcases and white sheets. I made all my beds up with the same width of sheet turned down over the blanket, all tucked in with hospital corners. My dormitory looked neat and tidy. I felt so proud and couldn't wait for the children to arrive.

Just after lunch the coach arrived. Mr Farrar brought the excited children round past the swimming pool and into the side door.

Mrs Farrar and Ann sorted the children out with a coat peg and shoe slot for outdoor shoes. It was my job to give all the children a pair of black plimsolls to wear indoors.

In the washroom the children also had a peg for their towel and washbag. Under supervision, the children went outside to explore after boundaries were explained. There were trees to climb, swings and things to play with. They wanted to do everything at once. It was lovely to watch them, the quiet ones taking a bit longer. Some had sisters with them.

After tea and more playing, the children went into the television room. They were called in age groups after supper and a drink, then a wash. The younger ones came first. Clothes were folded tidily, with slippers underneath the bed.

The two beds near the bottom of the dormitory, by the fire door, were taken by older children.

When morning came, children were encouraged to open up their beds to air whilst they got washed and dressed. This allowed us to discreetly check whether any beds needed to be changed later. The children then made an effort to tidy their beds and went down to the playroom for breakfast.

Mr and Mrs Farrar sat in the dining room with the children while staff ate together in another room.

After breakfast, depending on the weather, the children were either in the playroom, where there were lots of games, or outside with adults in attendance while the two dormitory people went to tidy beds, dust, mop the bedrooms, clean bathroom and toilets, then they would sweep and dry mop the long corridors. After this we went to play with children.

After lunch, depending on the weather, so many children at a time were allowed in the swimming pool until all who wanted to had been in.

After tea, the children were split into groups and for the rest of the holiday, with an adult, were taken walking round the area. Nine times out of ten I was the last one to arrive back.

On Sundays at teatime, Miss Heron used to travel from Beeston or Middleton with others. In the TV room we would have a little service singing hymns. Miss Heron would tell a story, relating it to a Bible story. Some of the children had been before and really enjoyed this time.

As time went on and I gained more confidence, when Miss Heron couldn't come I used to tell the story in turn with Mr Farrar. I still have a book Miss Heron gave me called 'The Queen's Muffin Man'.

Soon change over day would come. There were sad goodbyes. It was amazing how well we got to know children in such a short time. We would wave the children off, then got cracking – change and re-make all the beds, sweep, mop and disinfect everywhere so that everything was ship shape and welcoming for the next group.

We worked from 7 a.m. until 9 p.m. each day, although we did get one day off midweek. The salary was £5 a fortnight. If I went out one week I had to stay local the next week because there wasn't enough money left. I loved walking so I would take a sandwich, bring some sewing or knitting, and take myself off somewhere. I did enjoy my days off but couldn't wait to get back to the children.

In July 1961 on the change over Friday I went back to Leeds on the coach with the children. It was my 21st birthday and I wanted to spend it with my family. I returned on the Monday to carry on with my duties.

One year, a friend of Silverdale died – an author, William Riley. Some of the older children went to his funeral to represent Silverdale. They looked very smart in the Silverdale outfit with navy blue Burberry coats.

One thing I do remember well. On a Friday when the girls arrived, I was in my usual spot in the stores giving out pumps. The light in the room was not very good but I could just about see the shoe sizes. This girl came in. I asked her shoe size and found her a pair of pumps. She sat on the floor with her legs straight out in front of her, never bent her legs to put the pumps on. I thought her knees looked as if they had bandages on them. Later I asked Mrs Farrar if any information had been sent with regards to her care, thinking she had fallen and hurt her knees. Mrs Farrar said no, but had a chat with the girl. It turned out that she had two artificial legs that strapped on over her shoulders. Mrs Farrar was surprised she had been allowed to come. The girl was in my dormitory. She was so good - very independent, never complained. She just got on with everything. She would sit on her bed, take her limbs off and fasten them on the bottom of her bed. What a girl! She could run and climb trees with the best of them. I wonder where she is now?

Mr and Mrs Farrar were so good and easy to get on with. Uncle Harry, Mr Farrar's brother, used to come and stay and do odd jobs and some gardening. The children loved him to bits. What happy days – full of fun and laughter.

In those days you had to do what your parents said. Every year I would have a row with my father because I would give up my job and go back to Silverdale.

When I was seven years old my own mother died. My father married again but I was so unhappy. All I wanted to do was look after children and give them the happiness I had missed out on.

Because of my time at Silverdale I had the confidence to fulfil my dream. I went on to work at reception centres for Sheffield City Council and then moved on to Wandsworth, London, where I worked until I married and started my own family.
Margaret Bromley (nee Sayles)

In 1964, the Association's Jubilee Year, the Farrars resigned after eight years.

Mr and Mrs Andrew C Goodill took up duties as Warden and Matron, and were to stay for four years. Andrew Goodill had recently retired as a naval officer. Mrs Goodill was a State Registered Nurse. After their first year, they were confirmed in their opinion that the work gave them the opportunity to put their Practical Christianity into action. Commenting that we live in an increasingly materialistic age, Mr Goodill quoted Winston Churchill – 'What is the use of living if it be not to make this world a better place for those who will live in it after we are gone?'

They were happy to see so many children enjoying a holiday in magnificent surroundings. The benefit to the children was no longer judged in weight gained, but in improved health and appearance, the alertness teachers reported when children returned to school after a holiday, and in the eagerness with which places were sought – demand always exceeding availability.

Several 'old girls' and 'old boys' visited during the Goodills' first summer, including a married couple who had both been at the camp in 1905.

The mid 1960s brought high inflation and the Association continued throughout the sixties to appeal for subscribers and particularly for people willing to take out a covenant. As inflation continued to rise into the 1970s, expenses increased by 25%. But none of that ever concerned the children. In a brief note to the Yorkshire Evening Post, Charles Jennings said –

It was the thrill of my young life to set off on an adventure. I was absolutely captivated by the sunset over the bay. It was the most beautiful sight of my life.

Vicar of Silverdale, William Riley, Vicar's wife, Ernest and Phoebe Farrar

THE TIMES THEY ARE A-CHANGING

The practice of weighing children went on until the 1970s. What's more, the Bradford Cinderella Home decided, after sixty odd years of not doing so, that weighing kids was a terrific idea. In 1972, the Leeds Committee obtained a set of scales for the Cinderella Home from the Leeds & District Hospital fund. There's always been a touch of rivalry between Leeds and Bradford. Perhaps it is just as well that the Cinderella Home had not been weighing children from the earliest days or there may have been an end of season competition to see whose children were most plumped up.

Mr and Mrs E W Cauldwell of the Cinderella Home took over from the Goodills as Warden and Matron and stayed five years. They were succeeded by their son and daughter-in-law Mr and Mrs David Cauldwell, continuing the tradition of having a married couple in place and paying them a joint salary. Like many other practices, this would soon become a thing of the past.

I was there 1967, 1968. I loved it. As you get older, you look back. I'd not understood we were deprived as kids. My mum was a single parent, working all hours. We did come first.

I remember going to Silverdale and getting out of the pool and a helper coming out with a tray of lemon squash. I'd never heard of lemon squash. The second time I went, I knew that was lemon squash.

I remember the beds being clean, the dormitory clean. I felt safe. I felt cared for.

You knew that you were adequately dressed. I remember the cotton sweat shirts we wore. People made sure you were washed, dressed, your hair done.

I enjoyed the song and playing on the swings, in the pool, on the sandpit. The park for us at home was nearly a mile up a hill.

I remember having blancmange. I'd never heard of it, and have never had it anywhere else. I remember having loads of bread and butter on the table and bananas. You'd have a glass of milk at night with a biscuit. We never had that. We couldn't keep milk as we didn't have a fridge. We'd get one pint of milk a day and at night there'd be just enough left for Mum's cup of tea in the morning.

I always remember peeling an orange. If you peeled it in one you got a threepenny bit. I still can't do it, peel it in one. Every time I eat an orange, I think of Silverdale.

Lynne Higo

A HAPPY PARTY AT SILVERDALE

The 1974 boundary changes resulted in Leeds becoming geographically larger as it swallowed up surrounding small towns and villages into its administrative system. South Westmorland Rural District Council became part of the new County of Cumbria.

In 1977, Silverdale Youth Involvement Auxiliary Committee received £10,000 from the Queen's Silver Jubilee Appeal to encourage young people to help others less fortunate than themselves. SYIAC brought energy, enthusiasm and practical help. SAM, Silverdale Associate Members, undertook to donate the sum of £10 annually by donation or through organising an event.

For the 75th anniversary celebrations in 1978, the young people visited camp for the first time and took with them the 'Slack & Tight Minstrels' who performed for the children. They helped to take some of the first campers back on a nostalgic visit to Silverdale.

These young people from more privileged backgrounds admirably expected less privileged children to have the same standards of comfort that they enjoyed themselves. They visited the camp during a chilly spell.

They said it was too cold at the camp, and not much of an excuse that the heating system was playing up. Children needed a milky drink at night. They should wear pumps indoors and not go about in stockinged feet. Bed-wetters should have mattresses and pillows with an inner plastic case. In the era of Cadbury's Smashed potato - *for Mash, get Smash!* – the Silverdale Youth Committee had severe comments about the camp diet. This stung the senior committee members who had never had complaints about the food before.

The children of 1910 could have done with a Youth Involvement Committee to do a bit of stirring. In those early years, one poor lad died of pneumonia a few days after coming home. (The committee recorded the fact that he had gone back to school for two days after returning from Silverdale. So that was all

Courtesy of Y.E.P.

right then.) What would they have made of the year 1923, when children in the poorest of physical health continued their holidays into November?

The young people's caring, humanitarian approach was also seen among committee members in the early seventies. Reception and departure had always led to debates about how best and where to arrange it. Some committee members worried that women and children were waiting in the street without shelter and that some children may have become upset. For the first time, children began to travel to camp in their own clothing and to change into camp clothes the following day.

Though great changes have taken place over the years, the original 1904 Constitution stayed in place until 1983, when it was rewritten by the late Roddie McLeod.

The worst year for everyone involved was 2001 when, for the first time since the 1919 fire, the camp did not open. There were two reasons for this. The Foot and Mouth Epidemic meant that the countryside was 'closed'. Foot-paths and many outside attractions were out of bounds. A difficult problem regarding staff led to changes and the introduction of some new procedures.

The Holiday Centre re-opened in March 2002 under a new management team. During that season, 249 children enjoyed a holiday, compared to 278 in 2000.

The titles Superintendent, Warden and Matron are no longer used. There is now an Officer in Charge and a Deputy. The first person with the title Officer in Charge was Jane Carter. After many years of service in other roles, she succeeded in a competitive interview for the post at the end of 2001. Much of the success of that 'comeback season' was down to Jane.

The Association's title has changed since its beginnings. Originally Leeds Poor Children's Holiday Camp, the word 'Poor' disappeared from the front cover of the Annual Report in 1949 only to reappear in 1952, just for that one year. From 1966 to 1991 the wording on the front cover said that the Camp was for 'needy and underprivileged children.' That wording stayed until 1992 when it changed to 'For children in need since 1904'.

There were many 'firsts' during the seventies, eighties and nineties. New legislation required supervisory staff to have training before the annual opening. Domestic staff also required training in modern hygiene methods. The ratio of staff to children was increased. The Children Act led to even closer involvement with the local authority, including the implementation of annual inspections. The authority's inspection reports have on the whole been highly complimentary.

The Lady Mayoress has traditionally taken on the role of President. The first female Lord Mayor also took on that role in 1974.

The camp received its first colour TV in April 1978, – donated by Mr Julian Vallance – 'a boon in inclement weather'. (Its first black and white TV had been donated by Leeds University students in the 1950s).

In August 1988, natural gas came to Silverdale – though there is still no mains sewerage system.

In 1983 mixed parties of boys and girls coming to camp together proved a great success. When brothers and sisters could attend together, this diminished feelings of homesickness. The word 'stress' appeared for the first time in the 1978 Annual

Report, as another reason for children needing a holiday – a break in routine.

Stress also perhaps became a greater factor for the staff during this period as noted in a meeting of June, 1989. 'The last party of children to visit the camp caused the warden a great deal of worry, and some sleepless nights. He had to bring one girl back to Leeds the day after she arrived, because of incessant swearing and smoking in the dormitory.'

Vera Ferguson, Assistant Secretary to the Association for fourteen years until her retirement at the age of 74 in 1992, has seen many changes. She used to send sixty or so children a fortnight and it did her heart good to see them coming back so healthy and rosy and asking to go again the following year. She praises former Secretaries - Harry Atkinson (1981 to 1984), Terry Clark (1984 to 1997) and Kathleen Turner, who put in such good work over the years. Vera, still active on the Committee, comments on an expense that has arisen since her day – rent. 'With it being a charity, the corporation gave us an office in Portland Crescent and it was rent-free. Now rent is £6,000 a year, and that makes a big difference to a small charity.'

Joan Kershaw, Committee member, helped Vera for many years and continues to help Christine Masterman on a regular basis when children and their parents come into the office each Tuesday, for a briefing before going to the camp the following week.

Lord Mayor Councillor Mrs Rose Lund named Silverdale as one of her benefiting

charities 1986-87. The founders would have recognised some of the charity events that took place during the 1980s, and they would be astonished by others. The events included a beer lorry push from Harrogate to Leeds. A balloon race was held in Roundhay Park. Many balloons were caught in the trees, some valves did not work, but one balloon made it all the way to Switzerland. There was a sponsored swim; donations from Kirkstall Gala; a sponsored Lyke Wake walk; parachute jumps, including one by Lady Mayoress Mrs Joan Vollans in 1988; fashion shows, coffee mornings, concerts by East Leeds Labour Club; Children in Need Appeal; 'Sponsored Toddle' at Hunslet Nursery School as well as Open Day and Flag Day; Leeds Printers' Gala and Leeds Community Chest awards; a Joe Johnson snooker event and a clay pigeon shoot. A particular coup for the Association was the April 1981 charity match between Leeds United and Burussian Dortmund, arranged by the Rotary Club.

For ten years, committee members Brooke Nelson and his wife Joan have organised a hugely successful dinner dance in early spring, for several years at the Irish Centre, York Road and latterly at the North-West Liberal Club in Woodhouse.

However, perhaps the most remarkable feat of fund-raising in recent years was that of former Chairman Eric Forster (1990-92) who in 1999 contributed a cheque for £10,000 which he had raised by charging £25 to £50 for talks about the camp and other topics. How much work was that!

During the year 1991-92 I was the President of Soroptimist International of Leeds. As I was a Primary School Head Teacher before I retired, I chose the Leeds Children's Holiday Camp as the club charity for the year. The members happily agreed.

At my school brothers and sisters had queued up to go to Silverdale. The camp provided a good healthy holiday, also giving them a little independence. They used to return suntanned and rosy cheeked. At Harvest Festival time our tinned and dried food was sent to the camp HQ where it was stored for the following year.

The Soroptimists held a Christmas Street Collection in Dortmund Square, and also an evening of flower arranging, demonstrated by George Smith.

Our 'Forties Evening' opened with the 'Air Raid Siren' and ended with the 'All Clear'. Everyone attended in wartime uniforms and entry was by ticket – a Soldier's Service Pay Book, designed by Margaret Dixon using her late husband's army pay book. Our own members provided the cabaret – The Andrew Sisters, Marlene Dietrich and a friend who impersonated George Formby.

Another popular evening was a concert – music provided by the Yorkshire Police Band and St Raphael Singers.

The charity was popular with everyone. In all we raised £3,500 and contributed many gifts of clothing.

Mary Smith

Courtesy of Y.E.P.

Leeds City Council remains the major supporter of the Association. Several council leaders have proved good friends to Silverdale. The Council is committed to inspections of the holiday premises under the Children Act, without which inspections and approval the Camp would not function. Over the years the Council's expertise and advice have helped the Association to modernise the holiday centre. As a small charity, with only one part-time paid member of staff in the Leeds office, the Association needs and values its relationship with the Council.

For many years the Council allowed the Association to have land outside Elland Road. This was operated as a car park and helped finances enormously. In 1996 during the build up to the European Championships, police advised the Council to rationalise its car parking. The car park operated by the Association, along with others, was 'bought out' for a considerable sum.

Financial support from the Council represents a crucial part of the Association's funding, at around £40,000 per year.

Three people at the heart of the Association today are Alan Pinder, Chairman since 1992 and Treasurer since 1981, Vice Chairman L Grenville Fletcher and Secretary Christine Masterman.

Grenville Fletcher first became aware of LCHA via a colleague while a member of Leeds City Council. He was invited to join the Committee in September 1986 and became Vice Chairman in 1990. Since he retired from business in Leeds in 1997 he has worked in the office several days a week, mainly attempting to raise funds for various camp projects. He visits the camp regularly, and for the staff he is 'like a breath of fresh air'.

I joined L.C.H.A. in February 1993 as Assistant Secretary working two mornings a week. At that time the holidays were two weeks with the first group going in March and two weeks later the next group left. So one group arrived at 12.0 midday and the next group left at 1.0p.m this was all the way through the season till September each year, taking 40 children at a time.

Later we changed to eleven days giving staff the weekend off. This worked well but started a decline in numbers. More families do have holidays so therefore they will not send children to us. Eventually we were given a mini-bus by the Variety Club and we now take 12 children at a time Monday to Friday, this is working well and the children prefer the five days and the different outings especially on the trains and doing things they do not do at home.

Some of the Head Teachers and School Mentors do contact the office to know more about us and I hope we have a good working relationship.

The most satisfying part of my job is when the children return home on a Friday and they say that they have had a wonderful time and can they go next year. The older ones say that they wish they could go again.

Working for the LCHCA has been and still is the most satisfying work I have ever done in my working career.

Christine Masterman

Alan Pinder looks forward to the centenary celebrations in a mood of uncertainty.

'In many ways 2002 was an amazing year in the history of the Association, and 2003 threatens to equal it. The rate of change is quite astonishing, but so far the Trustees are just managing to stay ahead of the game.'

'It was at the end of the season when a number of factors caused the Trustee Board to look closely once again at the nature of our product. First of all, the Association was very short of money. This was nothing new, but the Shell Shares had to be sold, in September 2002, and only the very large legacy left by the late Miss Barbara Snape enabled the Association to see out the year.

'Secondly, there had again been "market resistance" to our holidays which could not all be put down to the SATS, or lack of publicity, or any other excuse. The fact was that City Council officers, teachers, parents and most importantly the children themselves all considered the holidays to be too long. Therefore it was decided from March 2003 to introduce a new FIVE days' holiday, only FOUR days in weeks where there is a Bank Holiday on Monday. There would be a maximum of 12 children per week. However, the holidays were to be packed with outings, trips, etc, to tire the children out and to hide the fact that we cannot quite run to a "Gameboy" for every child!

'At the time of writing (May 2003) the shorter holidays have been a tremendous success with positive reactions from all the parties referred to above. There are clear physical and financial benefits, many arising out of the fact that all trips to and from Leeds are now done by the new mini-bus, driven by our own staff, with a tremendous reduction in costs.

'Of course, many people including our own supporters will feel it difficult to reconcile themselves to the fact that a dozen or so children now rattle around in the space where little more than ten years ago there were fifty or even sixty! But the camp was designed and built to meet physical needs of under-privileged children from what were then urban slums. There are still needy children in Leeds, but that need is now largely emotional, and far more subtle and difficult to cater for.'

Alan Pinder
Annual Report

The Association has reached its centenary year still giving free holidays at Silverdale to children in Leeds, but Alan says that he cannot forecast the future, and believes that perhaps it is best not to try. There is disappointment in the office that the bid for funding from Children in Need has been turned down.

CAMP SONG

(official version!)

There is a happy Camp at Silverdale,

Where we all go for walks, down the lane,

The wishing well we have seen,

The Pepper Pot and the village green

And we are happy kids at Silverdale.

Our camp is far away LCHCA

Where we have lovely food, 3 times a day,

3 warm blankets for our bed

And a pillow for our head

And we are happy kids at Silverdale.

Soon the time will come to say "Bye Silverdale"

Where we all enjoyed walks down the lane,

We shall not forget the staff,

The fun and games and jolly laughs,

3 cheers for happy days at Silverdale.

Hip Hip Hooray.

Silverdale is not just a place on the map. To the thousands of children who have spent happy days there during the years, it's a name they will never forget.

May it long continue to be so.

Ernest H. Morris

Chairman until his death in 1989

TODAY AND TOMORROW

On a fine Friday in March 2004, I set off from Leeds to take another look at the Leeds Poor Children's Holiday Camp of my childhood. The roller coaster B6254 shoots off from the A65, leading to Carnforth. From there it's a straight run to Silverdale. Missing the turn-off for the camp, I buy a pint of milk in the shop where generations of Leeds children have bought sweets, then wind my way back across forty odd years.

The red sign names Leeds Children's Holiday Centre. A hand-written notice posted in well-kept grounds announces Saturday car boot sales – proceeds to the Holiday Centre.

A couple of Thunderbird cars squat near the front of the building: the Scimitar car club are here for the weekend.

Most places are smaller than you remember. This is still big and impressive. Later, Stephen Metcalfe, the caretaker who really does take magnificent care of the grounds, will tell me that the building has been surveyed recently. It has stood for near on fifty years and will be good for another fifty. Only the flat roof needs attention.

I can't see the pool where I learnt to swim. There's a modern structure that looks as if it houses saunas for stressed-out executives. This turns out to be the swimming pool, housed in a wooden chalet.

Through the kitchen window, workmen spot me loitering and open a side door. I walk through a bare corridor in need of decoration. Because the rooms are to be occupied by Scimitar enthusiasts, I'm in the office with the goldfish and will sleep on the bottom bunk in the First Aid room.

Linda Watts, Officer in Charge, shows me round. Through her eyes I see what the corridor will look like when it is redecorated and the pictures are back on the walls. She shows me round cosy dormitories cubicled off for privacy so that children can share or have their own little room.

The views from the public rooms are breathtaking. Memory or change of use has shifted things about. The dining room seems to be the place where we put on our pantomimes. I look at the big clock and remember the little girl saying, 'What time is it?' 'What time is it now?' 'What time is it?'

Throughout the history of the Camp, there has been a Silverdale Local Committee. That evening, I talk to Alan Tomlinson, its Chairman. The Committee has 'a capable and long standing Treasurer and a new Secretary, together with two new enthusiastic members'.

Alan recalls Civic Days when children gave concerts in the big hall with views over the sea and Morecambe Bay, and children singing 'He's Got the Whole World in His Hands'. 'Almost always there was sunshine,' Alan says.

As a Methodist, he regrets that the children now come only Mondays to Fridays because he enjoyed taking part with the children in the Sunday services held at the Methodist Church.

What does the future hold? It is difficult for Alan to speak of the future of the organisation, especially because finance is now a great problem. 'The Association must comply with many new laws concerning fire, safety, hygiene, minimum wage and especially very heavy insurance premiums. Costs have to be incurred with staff credentials needing to be checked, and this alone is quite expensive. I believe that applications have been made to both the Lottery and to the fund Children in Need, all to date without success.'

Alan respects the present management. He has known Linda Watts for many years. 'She is doing a first class job in conjunction with an excellent staff, not forgetting the groundsman Stephen Metcalfe who has made many improvements to the gardens and the lawn areas.'

Linda Watts has brought her own style to the camp. She lives in the village. This is a first. All previous camp officers have lived on the premises. The mother of two girls, she worked as a supervisor at the camp for a year in 1985, when there were sixty children and three supervisors. Her colleague, Irene Doyle, started around four years ago – and did two years on nights.

Working nights was spooky at first, Linda and Irene agreed. Pipes bang and rattle. If a child couldn't sleep and came quietly up behind you and reached out a hand, you'd scream. One night, Irene counted heads. One missing. She counted again. She looked in all the rooms, then rang David – 'One's gone missing!' They searched. The girl was sitting at the dining room table, eyes wide open. They led the sleepwalker back to bed.

Sometimes at night, it could be hard to get the children to sleep. They'd sit and talk to them, make them laugh, give them a teddy bear and say, 'Pretend it's your mum and give her a big hug.'

In the morning, they'd say, 'How's your mum?'

'She's fine. I slept like a log.'

At night those in charge clean up, bake, get breakfast ready and change the beds if children have an accident. Children's clothes are washed every night, dried and back on each locker next morning.

Almost every girl who comes now has head lice. They handle this tactfully and with humour, though my head starts to itch as they explain. 'Let's have a look what friends you've got today.' They put on treatment for the week. One girl was riddled. Lice were eating her head. They managed to clear it up but thought they might have to take her to the doctor. On such a tight budget, they can't really afford these expensive treatments.

Linda spins the money skilfully. They give the children a good holiday. If it's someone's birthday, there's a party and presents. Some of the children have never had a party before, and never had a cake.

The advantage of having smaller groups is that they can be taken on trips every day, on a train ride, to the bird sanctuary, the butterfly house, to the sands at Morecambe and out bowling. With big groups there was effing and blinding on the trips and people complained. Twelve is a good number these days when children do not naturally take to walking in a crocodile and minding their Ps and Qs.

The children love the swimming pool.

In the evening children read or play. Books are changed every year because some children return again and again. They watch television in a cosy room with nibbles, crisps and a glass of milk – have a treat.

In 1914 the Camp was offered as a hostel for Belgian refugees. In 2004, several children of Leeds-based asylum seekers are enjoying holidays at the Camp.

Linda runs the camp as her own kids would like it. Civic Days have changed too. Over the years on Civic Day the children have eaten in the dining room and visitors lunched on their way to Silverdale. Last year children sat with the grown ups and after the meal showed them round. Everyone enjoyed it.

Linda has a little blazer that was once part of the camp uniform. Now children wear Reebok, Man United, Liverpool and Leeds shirts. Sometimes a child is sent home with a prized item of clothing.

Most of the children just need a good holiday. But there must always have been children whose impoverishment had deeper roots. Perhaps also we are more aware now of children with attention deficit disorders or behavioural problems.

'One boy was so helpful when he was all right, the nicest lad you could meet, but then might suddenly go off the rails. Staff would have to get him to one side and calm him down,' Linda says.

Stephen occasionally has the task of taking children home if they are too disruptive. 'You need a lot of patience and have to be adaptable.'

On Saturday, when car booters in the grounds wait for customers and Scimitar club members take joy in classical lines and polished bodywork, I walk to the Pepper Pot. My guide is Tasha, Linda's ten year old daughter. We walk through Holgates Caravan Park into ancient Eaves Wood.

The Pepper Pot is a stone tower built in 1887 to commemorate the Golden Jubilee of Queen Victoria. Generations of children have visited and remembered this local landmark. I remember walking through the woods. I remember Mr Farrar becoming alarmed when I put something in my mouth – until he saw that it was just a shiny round blade of grass. I have no recollection of the Pepper Pot, though I am sure we must have visited it. I was probably plotting the intricacies of our 'Jack and the Beanstalk' finale, or wondering how best to dramatise the moment when Sleeping Beauty opens her eyes and leaps into her happily ever after life.

I would not have found my way to the Pepper Pot without Tasha, and tell her so. If she's not sure of the way, she tells me, she stops, looks at the trees, grass and stones, and then she knows the way.

Tasha makes friends with the children who come to the camp. She taught herself to swim in the pool and likes it in the summer when there is lots to do. Sometimes she writes to children, but you don't know what to say after a while. Tasha likes playing football as a centre striker and goes to athletics once a week. 'Silverdale is a nice place because like when you go on holiday there's loads to do. It's got walks and things and the local village and stuff, and all the trips.' Tasha enjoys it, even though she lives here. She thinks the children who come enjoy it, but it depends on what kind of person they are, because they might not want to enjoy it.

We reach the Pepper Pot, admire the view and take each other's photograph. Nearby are the giant's footsteps. Tasha tries one out for size.

We sit down for a rest and she tells me a story. 'I heard this story about the Pepper Pot off Amanda, one of the staff. There was a giant lived near the Pepper Pot and he had two slaves, and they say there is pepper in the Pepper Pot and the slaves always used to take pepper to the giant. But I don't know whether it's true or not.'

I'm sure her story's true. If four people in Leeds can come up with an idea and start a holiday adventure that lasts for a hundred years, anything is possible.

THE LAST WORD

Silverdale has swings and I'm their biggest fan.

I like the pool because you can splash about and splash other people around.

We have nice beds what are called dormitories. They're good because we don't have to share a room.

I mistakenly bumped into a friend and I did not look at the track in front and crashed but still I come in second.

We go out places that are really cool and we have fun; thirther-more we get to miss school and that is great.

The staff are wonderful. Their names are Russell, Amanda, Oliver and Hayley.

I went to the bird sanctuary and I brought my binoculars. I saw lots of birds.

The food is wonderful. We get deserts.

I like Silverdale Children's Holiday Camp because they don't waste food, they give it to Linda's hens.

Trips are cool, we go Go-Karting and Bowling.

I like it when you make new friends at Silverdale.